MY DISNEY

STARS AND HEROES 5

Student's Book with eBook

Hawys Morgan

Scope and Sequence

Meet our Stars and Heroes!
page 4

Character introductions
I'm from … *I want …*
I enjoy … *I travel …*
I have … *My favorite …*

	Vocabulary	Grammar and communication	Personal and Social Skills	Cross-curricular	Writing project and strategies
1 Growing and changing page 10 	**Personality adjectives** Characteristics Capabilities	*What was he like when he was five? He was friendly. What are you like now?* **Ask and answer about ability in the past** *Could you tie your shoelaces when you were four? No, I couldn't.*	**Self-management:** Dealing with changes *I feel … because … You could write down your feelings.* **Story:** *The secret garden* (classic retelling)	**Science:** Migration *Africa, Asia, Central America, Europe, kilometers, migrate* **Mini-project** A migration fact file	An autobiography **Self-management:** Using a timeline
2 Healthy body, healthy mind page 22 	**Parts of the body** Illnesses Health advice	*What's the matter? My ankle hurts. I have a cold. I feel dizzy.* **Give advice for health problems** *You should see a doctor. She shouldn't go to basketball practice.*	**Responsible decision-making:** Identifying information you can trust *We can/can't trust this because … We shouldn't believe the information here.* **Story:** *The lazy lion and the fox* (fable)	**Science:** Healthy brains and routines *enough sleep/water, glucose, good diet, healthy routine, screen time* **Mini-project** A healthy routine	An advice column **Collaboration:** Group problem-solving
3 Technology for the future page 34 	**Technology at home** Technology More technology	*Will we have robotic teachers? Yes, we will. / No, we won't. We will ride electric motorcycles.* **Make predictions about the future** *What will schools be like? There will be artificial food.*	**Responsible decision-making:** Making good choices *The pros/cons are … This is better/worse for the environment.* **Story:** *The gift* (science fiction)	**Technology:** Eco-technologies *bioplastic, composting toilet, smart fridge, solar panel, water tank, wind turbine* **Mini-project** Eco-technology for school	A descriptive text **Presentation skills:** Using visuals and digital tools
4 Curious and creative! page 46 	**Adjectives** Food and taste adjectives Ingredients	*What does it look like? It smells horrible. It sounds like a bird.* **Describe quantity** *There's too much frosting. There aren't enough colors.*	**Social awareness:** Appreciating creativity *They aren't afraid to … What if we …? They know how to…* **Story:** *Charlie's creative cakes* (traditional story)	**Science:** Chemistry and food, *chemical reaction, gas, gel, irreversible/ reversible change, solid* **Mini-project** A creative meal	A blog post **Self-management:** Analyzing the task
5 Carnival fun! page 58 	**Carnival rides** Carnival activities More carnival activities	*We have to buy a ticket. You don't have to wait in line.* **Talk about how you feel about things** *He's scared of horror movies. What are you excited about?*	**Self-awareness:** Knowing what we value *I value … more than … I'm more interested in … The most important thing to me is …* **Story:** *A day at the carnival* (contemporary fiction)	**Engineering:** Rollercoasters *brakes, friction, gravity, loop, track, top* **Mini-project** A marble rollercoaster	An invitation **Collaboration:** Sharing responsibilities

Meet our Stars and Heroes!

Look, think, and wonder.

1. Do you know any of the characters?
2. Who would you like to meet?

1 **Read. Then play *Who am I?***

I like ice skating!

Are you Riley?

Mulan

W

MOVIE QUIZ

1. Where is Mulan from?
2. What does she want to be?

She can horseback ride and use a bow and arrow. She's smart and brave.

Alice

4

MOVIE QUIZ

1. Where does Alice travel to?
2. Who is her good friend?

She likes traveling to new places. Her good friend the Mad Hatter creates awesome hats.

Belle

7

MOVIE QUIZ

1. Where does Belle live?
2. What does the Beast look like?

She's smart and she loves reading. At the start, she thinks the Beast is scary, but they become good friends.

Riley

1

MOVIE QUIZ

1. Where does Riley move to?
2. What's her favorite sport?

She loves ice skating with her family. She learns to love her new home in San Francisco.

Rapunzel

2

MOVIE QUIZ

1. Where does Rapunzel live?
2. What's special about her hair?

She can use her long hair for climbing! She learns who she can trust.

Elastigirl

3

MOVIE QUIZ

1. What is Elastigirl's superpower?
2. How many people are in her family?

I'm Elastigirl! I'm, you know, flexible.

Her family are Supers with special powers. Her real name is Helen Parr.

Joe

8

MOVIE QUIZ

1. Which city does Joe live in?
2. What musical instrument does he play?

I'm going to live every minute of it.

He loves playing the piano. He thinks playing music for a band is the most important thing in the world.

Woody

5

MOVIE QUIZ

1. What kind of toy is Woody?
2. Who is his new friend?

That makes you a very important toy.

He's a toy who's brave and loyal. He values his friends.

Russell

9

MOVIE QUIZ

1. What does Russell wear?
2. Who does Russell try to help?

I'm a Wilderness Explorer.

He travels with Carl in a flying house. He gets a new badge when he learns a new skill.

Ian

6

MOVIE QUIZ

1. Who does Ian want to meet?
2. What's his brother's name?

Whatever it takes, I'm going to meet my dad!

He has an unusual pet – a small dragon! He learns to drive a car.

2 **Do the movie quizzes.**

3 **Talk about movies with a friend.**

1. Which character do you think is the most like you? Why?
2. Which movie are you most looking forward to watching? Why?
3. Which character quote do you like the best? Why?

W Welcome!

Who are our heroes?

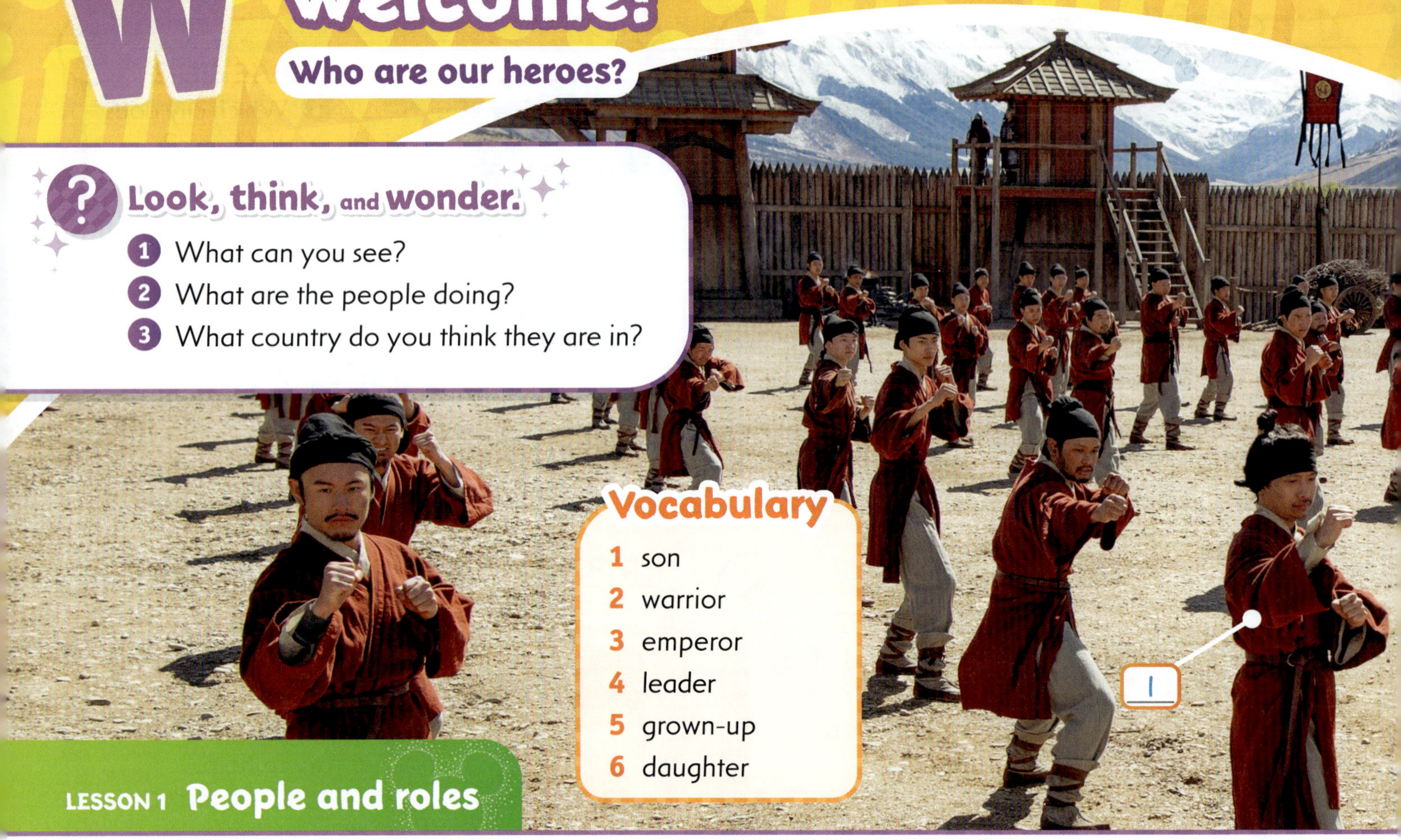

Look, think, and wonder.

1. What can you see?
2. What are the people doing?
3. What country do you think they are in?

Vocabulary

1. son
2. warrior
3. emperor
4. leader
5. grown-up
6. daughter

LESSON 1 People and roles

1 **Match the words to the pictures. Then listen, check, and repeat.** (0.1)

→ Which words describe you?

Storyboard Disney MULAN

2 **Watch the video. Write *T* (True) or *F* (False).** (0A)

1. Mulan is a son. F
2. Mulan's parents have three daughters. ____
3. Mulan is a grown-up. ____
4. She isn't a warrior. ____
5. The emperor is a leader. ____

3 **Describe Mulan to a friend.**

Mulan was a warrior.

I can use words that describe people.

LESSON 2 Simple past with *ago*

1 Watch the video again and answer.

Being a good leader

1. How was Commander Tung a good leader?
2. Mulan's father says, "*The leader became a legend.*" How is Mulan a good leader?
3. Do you think you are a good leader?

Relationship skills

2 Read, think, and say with a friend.

Grammar Heroes page 118

What did she do an hour ago?
She rode a horse an hour ago.

3 Read and complete.

1. Where (do) ___did___ Mulan live many years ago?
2. She (live) ______________ in China many years ago.
3. Mulan's father (help) ______________ the emperor several years ago.
4. They (work) ______________ in a small village a few months ago.

4 Ask and answer with a friend.

What did you do a week ago?

I went to the new swimming pool.

I can ask and answer about when things happened in the past.

LESSON 3

Tag questions

This character loves gymnastics.

Is it Emily?

1 Read and play *Guess who!* Then do the quiz.

Pablo

I wrote a play script for my drama club!

QUIZ
Who does Pablo go geocaching with in Unit 9?

He loves reading and acting.
He can snowboard.

Emily

I love trying new things!

QUIZ
What's the name of the band Emily reviews in Unit 8?

She loves gymnastics and music.
She likes adventures.

Ash

I write for the school magazine!

QUIZ
What unusual ice cream does Ash try in Unit 4?

He enjoys cooking for his family.
He cares about healthy living.

Flo

I want to protect the environment.

QUIZ
Who does Flo help in the escape room in Unit 6?

She loves science fiction and technology.
Her favorite food is noodle soup.

2 0.2 Listen and read. Where are they going to go tomorrow?

Let's do our famous leaders project together. **Flo**

I think the best place to start is the city museum, don't you? **Pablo**

Yes! There's an exhibition about leaders, isn't there? **Emily**

Yes, there is. I saw a poster for it two days ago. Let's go tomorrow! **Ash**

I want to research Mahatma Gandhi and Nelson Mandela. **Pablo**

They're 20th century leaders, aren't they? **Flo**

Yes! OK, see you all in the morning! **Emily**

3 Look. Underline the question tags.

Grammar Heroes page 118

We can meet at the museum tomorrow, can't we?
I don't have to bring food, do I?
They can't take photos here, can they?
He is the emperor, isn't he?

4 Complete the tag questions. Then ask and answer.

1 Mulan is a warrior, ___isn't she___?
2 The Emperor is the leader, ______________?
3 Mulan can horseback ride, ______________?
4 Mulan's parents don't have a son, ______________?

I can ask and answer using tag questions.

FAMOUS LEADERS

1 Listen and read. Write the numbers.

66,000,000 years ago

_______ years ago

_______ years ago

_______ years ago

Tip

1,000 = a thousand
1,500 = one thousand five hundred
1,000,000 = a million

2 Order the leaders from youngest to oldest. Tell a friend.

3 Play *Guess who?*

I was an Egyptian queen. I lived about 2,000 years ago.

You're Cleopatra, aren't you?

I can use numbers 1,000 to 1,000,000.

1 Growing and changing

How do we deal with changes?

Look, think, and wonder.

1. How are Riley and her mom and dad feeling?
2. What activities can you see in the pictures?
3. Where do you think the people are?

1 (1.1) **Match the words to the pictures. Then listen, check, and repeat.**

→ Which words describe you?

Vocabulary

1 caring
2 naughty
3 talkative
4 shy
5 sporty
6 confident

I can use adjectives to describe personality.

Storyboard

2 Watch the video and answer.

Dealing with changes

1. What was the big change in Riley's life?
2. Why is Riley sad in San Francisco?
3. *"Everything is different now, but that's OK."* What do you think this means?

Self-management

3 Listen and write.

Riley lives with her 1 ___caring___ parents. She is a 2 ___________ young girl. When she was little, she was sometimes 3 ___________ . Riley is 4 ___________ . Ice skating is her favorite sport.

Then Riley and her family move to San Francisco. Riley feels 5 ___________ and sad at her new school. The other children are 6 ___________ , but she is quiet. Finally, Riley speaks with her parents, who understand and help her.

4 Tell your class what you are like.

I'm caring, confident, and sporty.

LESSON 2

Vocabulary

1 What words do you know for describing people?

physical appearance	hair	character
short	blond	sporty
handsome	curly	nice

2 Read and listen. Then match. (1.3)

Drama Club List of characters

We're going to act out a play at Drama Club. This is the character list. I want to be the prince!

❶ The King

He's handsome and **polite** – he always says "please" and "thank you." He's **patient** with the prince and princess. He doesn't get upset with them.

❷ The Princess

She's **unfriendly**. She isn't nice. She is always **impatient** with the king and queen. She wants everything NOW!

❸ The Prince

He's **lazy**. He doesn't like working. He's **dishonest**. He takes cookies from the baker's shop. By the end of the play, he changes. He tells the king about the cookies.

❹ The Baker

She's caring and **honest**. She tells the truth. She's **hardworking**. She works all day. By the end of the play, her life changes, but she doesn't.

Costumes

3 Write for you.

My friend is ____________ and ____________.

He / She isn't ____________ and ____________.

4 Describe and guess.

He's lazy and dishonest.

I know! It's the prince.

Talk buddies

If you can't guess, ask follow-up questions:

Is he/she (lazy)?

What does he/she look like?

I can use words for characteristics.

Disney · PIXAR INSIDE OUT

1 Watch, read, and circle.

1. Riley was (**friendly**) / **unfriendly** in Minnesota.
2. She isn't **shy** / **talkative** in San Francisco.
3. She's **patient** / **impatient** with her parents.
4. She feels sad when she's being **dishonest** / **honest**.

2 Watch again. Read and match.

1. What was Riley like when she was young? [b]
2. What was Riley like in San Francisco? [ ]
3. What is Riley like now? [ ]
4. What are Riley's parents like now? [ ]

a. They are caring and patient.
b. She was friendly, honest, and talkative.
c. She's sporty and happy.
d. She was sad, impatient, and dishonest.

3 Read, think, and say with a friend.

Grammar Heroes page 119

is / was + like				
What	was he	like when	he was	five?
He	was	friendly.		
What	are you	like now?		
I'm	confident.			

4 Ask and answer with a friend.

What were they like when they were seven?

They were lazy.

What are they like now?

They're sporty.

5 Write questions. Then ask a friend and write their answers.

What were you like when you were six?

What are you like now?

THE SECRET GARDEN

1 **Look at the story and answer.**

1 Can you describe the main character?
2 What makes the garden special?
3 Do you think this is a modern or a traditional story? Why?

2 1.4 **Listen and read. Compare Mary's old and new homes.**

Mary lived in India. When she was ten, her life changed. Her parents went to the hospital, but they never came home. Mary couldn't stay in India, so she **traveled alone** to England. Mary lives with her uncle now. His house is large and gray. She wants to be back in her colorful, warm house in India.

Martha works at the house. In the morning, she brings Mary her clothes. "I can't **tie my shoelaces**. Do it for me." says Mary. She isn't polite. "I could tie my shoelaces when I was six." says Martha. "You are ten. You do it. Don't be lazy."

Mary's uncle goes away. Mary explores the house and garden. One day, she finds a beautiful secret garden. She **does a cartwheel** in the grass. She feels happy here.

Think!

Where was Mary's uncle? Look and check your answers on page 119.

Mary sees Martha's brother, Dickon. He **whistles a tune**.
"Could you whistle when you were ten?" asks Mary.
"I could whistle when I was six. I can teach you."

One night, Mary sees a boy crying.
"I'm Colin. Who are you?" asks the boy. He's unfriendly and impatient.
"I'm Mary" she says. "We're cousins! Come – I want to show you my secret garden."
But Colin isn't well, and he can't walk.

Dickon and Mary take Colin outside. Colin feels stronger in the garden. Every day he tries to walk. What's Mary like now? She's patient and caring, like Martha.

A year later, Mary's uncle comes home. He finds Colin in the secret garden. He says, "Last year, you couldn't walk. Now you can. It's amazing! Thank you, Mary and Dickon."

3 Read again and write.

1 Where did Mary live before?
She lived in India.
2 Where does Mary live now?
____
3 Who is Mary's cousin?
____
4 Why is Mary's uncle happy at the end?
____

4 Vocabulary Write the correct verbs. Then match.

1 I can ____tie____ my shoelaces.
2 I can ____________ a cartwheel.
3 I can ____________ a tune.
4 I can ____________ alone.

a

b

c

d

5 Discuss with a friend.

Dealing with changes

1 How does Mary feel about change at the beginning of the story?
2 Who helps Mary deal with the changes in her life?
3 How do Mary and Colin change in the story?

Self-management

I can read a retelling of a classic novel about dealing with changes.

LESSON 5
Language focus

1 Listen and read. Who was confident? Who was sporty?

1.5

Hey Emily. Look at me when I was four!

Could you snowboard when you were four, Pablo?

Yes, I could. I was confident. What were you like when you were four?

I was sporty. I did gymnastics every week.

Could you do a cartwheel?

Yes, I could. Could you tie your shoelaces when you were four?

No, I couldn't. I learned when I was six.

Me too. Could you whistle a tune when you were six?

No, I couldn't. I still can't whistle a tune. But I can sing: la la la!

Stop!

2 Read again and circle.

1 Pablo **could** / **couldn't** snowboard when he was four.

2 Emily **could** / **couldn't** do a cartwheel when she was four.

3 Pablo **could** / **couldn't** tie his shoelaces when he was four.

4 Emily **could** / **couldn't** tie her shoelaces when she was six.

3 Read, think, and say with a friend. Find similar sentences in the dialog.

Grammar Heroes page 119

could / couldn't			
Could	you	tie your shoelaces	when you were four?
Yes, I could.			No, I couldn't.
She	could	do a cartwheel	when she was five.
He	couldn't	whistle a tune	when he was six.

Speak up!

4 Listen and repeat. Count the syllables. Underline the stressed syllables.

1.6

1 They were **unfriendly** when they were young. ____

2 He was **unkind** when he was young. ____

3 I was **impatient** when I was four. ____

5 Complete the questionnaire. Then ask and answer.

When you were five, could you ...

- do a cartwheel? ◯
- whistle a tune? ◯
- ____________ ◯
- ____________ ◯

Could you do a cartwheel when you were five?

No, I couldn't.

I can ask and answer about ability in the past.

Extra Lesson

Go online Phonics

Dealing with changes

1 How do characters in the unit deal with changes?

2 Read and write. Then listen and check. 1.7

Asking questions | Feeling angry | ~~Hiding from change~~ | Positive thinking

Dealing with changes

People deal with change in different ways. Here are four ways we deal with change.

1 Hiding from change

We don't want to believe that the change is happening. We hide from it because we're scared.

2 ______________

We try to find a way to stop the change from happening. We feel angry, sad, and impatient.

3 ______________

We ask questions about what's happening. We're worried, but also excited about the change.

4 ______________

We feel confident about the change. It's a little scary, but we feel happy, too.

How can we deal with the more negative feelings?

- **Keep a journal:** write your feelings in it.
- **Do research:** find out about life after the change.
- **Talk:** talk to your family and friends about how you feel.
- **Think positively:** think about the good things about the change.

3 Choose one of the changes below. Imagine how you feel. Which strategies can you use? Make notes.

Useful Language
I feel scared/worried/angry because …
You could find out more/talk to/write down …

You are moving to a new city.

You are starting a new school.

You are traveling alone for the first time.

I feel scared and angry – I don't want to move. I could find out more about the new city.

4 Find a friend who chose the same change. Share your ideas.

I'm moving to a new city. I feel angry.

Me too. I'm going to talk to my parents about how I feel.

Reflect
How can you help a friend deal with a difficult change?

Self-management I can learn to deal with changes.

Science

Migration

1 Read, listen, and answer.

1.8

1 Name a change that makes animals migrate.
2 Name an animal that migrates across the ocean.
3 Why do elephants and zebras migrate?

Reading strategy
Read large numbers by breaking them up into hundreds and thousands.
For example, 1,600: *one thousand six hundred.*

2 Vocabulary Read and complete.

Animals 1 ___migrate___ when the weather changes, to find food, or to have babies. Some birds live in 2 ______________ in the spring and summer, and fly to 3 ______________ in the fall. Every year, some turtles swim from 4 ______________ to 5 ______________ to have babies. Many animals travel for thousands of 6 ______________ every year.

3 Look and write the numbers. Which animals travel the longest distance?

birds __________ sea turtles __________

elephants __________

Migration: animals move from place to place, too!

Animals go through many changes. One of the biggest changes is when animals **migrate**.

Why do animals move from one place to another?

Sometimes animals migrate because of the change in weather. Sometimes they migrate to find more food. Other times animals migrate to have babies safely.

These hardworking birds live in **Europe** in the spring and summer. It's warm, so there are a lot of insects for the birds to eat. They build nests and have babies. In the fall, the weather changes. It's colder. There aren't many insects. It's time to migrate to a very different place – **Africa**! They prepare by eating a little more and getting into groups.

These tiny birds can travel an amazing 9,000 **kilometers**! It takes about six weeks. In the spring, they return to Europe.

Disney In the real world

When Riley moves from Minnesota to San Francisco she has to learn to deal with changes in her life. Like Riley, animals also have to deal with changes when they migrate from place to place.

I can read and understand about migration.

These sea turtles migrate from **Central America** to **Asia**. Every year, they migrate to the same beaches. They hide their eggs in the sand. Then they swim back across the ocean to find food. Some turtles migrate more than 12,000 kilometers.

In Africa, there are dry seasons and wet seasons. In the dry season, there isn't a lot of water or food. Large animals like elephants and zebras migrate across the grassland looking for water and grass. Large numbers of animals walk together. They travel more than 1,600 kilometers.

1 1.9 **Listen. How did Chinese mitten crabs first travel to new places?**

2 1.10 **Listen again and complete.**

Listening strategy

Read the word pool before you listen. Then listen out for key details which relate to the words.

Asia Europe kilometers migrate ~~shy~~

Migration Fact File

Name: Chinese mitten crabs

What are they like?

They are **1** ___shy___ animals.

Migration:

They first lived in **2** ______________. Now, you can also find them in **3** ______________ and the United States.

In the summer, they **4** ______________ to the ocean.

They can travel 18 **5** ______________ a day.

Interesting fact:

They grow new shells when they get bigger.

MINI-PROJECT

3 Design a migration fact file.

THINK What animals migrate to and from your country?

PLAN Choose and research an animal that migrates.

Workbook page 12

SHARE Present your fact file to the class.

I can design an animal migration fact file.

LESSON 9

Writing project

An autobiography

1 Read and write.

1 Who wrote the text? ____________

2 What's the text about? ____________

3 What's the writer like? ____________

____

2 Read again. Number the events in order.

a swim [ ]

b do a cartwheel [1]

c whistle a tune [ ]

d ride a bike [ ]

My autobiography

by Pablo

I live with my mom, dad, and big sister, Anna. I'm confident and sporty.

When I was six, I could do a cartwheel. I could swim when I was seven. Now, I still go swimming with my family.

When I was eight, I couldn't ride a bike. My sister helped me. She is patient. Now, I can ride my bike to school. I don't go alone, I go with Anna.

This year, I want to learn to whistle a tune.

Writing focus

In an autobiography, you write about the important details of your life:

- where you were born
- the school you went to
- your achievements
- important memories

Let's write!

3 Write an autobiography.

Think Think about important changes in your life.

school | sports | hobbies | abilities | family | personality

When did it happen? | What happened first / next / last? | How old were you when it happened?

Get ready Work with a partner to answer these questions.

- What were you like before? What are you like now?
- What could you do when you were younger? What can you do now?

Plan and write Create a timeline and write your autobiography. **Workbook** page 13

Tip

Self-management: using timelines

Use timelines to organize and order your life events. Make notes on the key events and what age they happened. What came first, next, last? Then, use your timeline to create your full draft.

Age: 1 2 3 4 5 6 7 8 9 10

1 – walk; 4 – start school; 6 – tie my shoelaces; 9 – play guitar

I can write an autobiography.

You can do it!

1 Write. Then listen and circle. (1.11)

1 Could he do a cartwheel when ___he___ was three?
Yes, he could. / (No, he couldn't.)

2 Could you tie your shoelaces when you ______ six?
Yes, I could. / No, I couldn't.

3 Could she travel alone ______ she was seven?
Yes, she could. / No, she couldn't.

4 Could I whistle a tune when I ______ four?
Yes, you could. / No, you couldn't.

5 Could ______ speak English when they were five?
Yes, they could. / No, they couldn't.

2 Read and write. Use the words in parentheses.

1 What are you like now? (polite) I'm polite now.
2 What were they like when they were five? (lazy) ______
3 What was she like when she was eight? (honest) ______
4 What were you like when you were nine? (sporty) ______
5 What were you like when you were three? (impatient) ______

Let's talk! How do we deal with changes?

3 Tell a friend how you feel about changes now.

family friends school hobbies

Movie quiz

1 Where does Riley live at the start of the movie?
2 Which sport do Riley and her parents play in the new house?

I can ...

- use words related to personality ☐
- talk about what people were like and past ability ☐
- deal with changes ☐
- write an autobiography ☐

I completed Unit 1!

Go online
Big Project

2 Healthy body, healthy mind

How can we stay healthy?

Look, think, and wonder.

1. What can you see?
2. How do you think Flynn feels?
3. What do think Rapunzel is going to do next?

1 2.1 **Match the words to the pictures. Then listen, check, and repeat.**

→ Name three body parts that join to the arm.

Vocabulary

1 wrist
2 ankle
3 elbow
4 knee
5 shoulder
6 neck

I can use body words.

Disney
Tangled
Storyboard

2 Watch the video and answer. (2A)

Following advice

1. Is Mother Gothel Rapunzel's mom?
2. Why does Mother Gothel want Rapunzel to stay in the tower?
3. Mother Gothel says, *"Trust me, my dear."* Can Rapunzel trust her?

Responsible decision-making

3 Listen and write. (2.2)

Flynn looked at his hands. There was blond hair around his **1** ___wrists___ . He couldn't move his arms because hair was around his **2** ______________ and his **3** ______________ . He couldn't move his feet and **4** ______________ or his legs and **5** ______________ . He turned his **6** ______________ to look around the room. There was blonde hair everywhere!

4 **Think of an activity. Say the parts of your body you use.**

Painting! I use my elbow, wrist, and hand.

Vocabulary

1 What body parts do you know?

outside	inside
wrists	bones

2 Read and listen. Then match. 2.3

Hi! I'm the First Aid Student Rep at school. My mom's a nurse, and this is her advice for staying healthy.

Health tips for a healthy body

It's good to be healthy. You can do a lot of activities with your friends. But when we don't feel very well, we have to be careful and take care of ourselves. This means not doing things that make us feel worse.

★ Feel 1 **dizzy**?
★ Have a 2 **headache**?

Don't play on your computer.

★ Have a 3 **cold**?
★ Have a 4 **sore throat**?
★ Have a 5 **cough**?

Don't play outdoors.

★ Have a 6 **stomachache**?
★ Have a 7 **toothache**?
★ Feel 8 **sick**?

Don't eat any junk food.

Let's be healthy!

3 Write for you.

I never have a toothache.

I sometimes have a cold.

I never ______________________

I sometimes ______________________

I ______________________

4 Mime and guess.

Do you have a cough?

Talk buddies

Keep the game going by saying:

Can you guess?

Guess again!

Your turn!

I can use words for illnesses.

Disney
Tangled

1 Watch, read, and circle.

Rapunzel says, 1 "**What's** / **Who's** the matter?"

"I don't 2 **think** / **feel** good." says Flynn.

"Do you feel sick?" asks Rapunzel.

"No, but my 3 **neck** / **hand** hurts." says Flynn.

"And I have a sore 4 **wrist** / **ankle**."

"Don't worry," says Rapunzel. "I can help."

2 Watch again. Read and write *T* (True) or *F* (False).

1. Flynn feels sick. F
2. His shoulder hurts. ____
3. Rapunzel can help. ____
4. Flynn has a sore ankle. ____

3 Read, think, and say with a friend.

Grammar Heroes page 120

Talking about illness		
What's the matter?		
My	hand / ankle / wrist / knee	hurts.
I have a / an	stomachache / headache / earache / toothache / backache. cold / sore throat / cough.	
I feel I don't feel	dizzy / sick. good.	

4 Ask and guess with a friend.

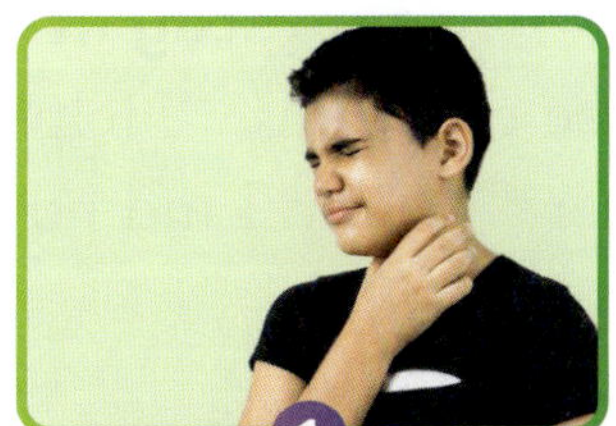
1

2

3

4

What's the matter?

I have a sore throat.

Picture 1!

Yes!

5 Choose and write a new dialog. Then act it out with a friend.

a cold a toothache feel dizzy knee hurts

What's the matter?
I have a toothache!

I can ask and answer about illnesses.

LESSON 4
Story

THE LAZY LION AND THE FOX

1 Look at the story and answer.

1 What do you think is the matter with the lion?
2 Who can you trust – the lion or the fox?
3 Do you think this is a modern story or a fable?

2 Listen and read. Does the lion feel sick?

Leo the lion is very lazy. Today, he has a stomachache. "I'm hungry," he says. "I need food, but I want to **stay in bed**." He sits under a tree and yells, "Help!".
"What's the matter?" asks a kind parrot.
"My tail hurts!" says Leo.
"Can I help?" asks the parrot.
"Come closer! Look at my tail."
The parrot flies down to help. Leo catches the parrot and puts her in his bag.
"Parrot for breakfast!" he laughs.
"What food can I find for lunch?"

"Help!" yells Leo.
"What's the matter?" asks a friendly monkey.
"I have a toothache," says Leo.
"Can I help?" asks the monkey.
"Come closer! Look in my mouth," says Leo. The monkey climbs down to help. Leo catches the monkey and puts him in his bag.
"Monkey for lunch!" he laughs.
"What food can I find for dinner?"
"Help!" yells Leo.
"What's the matter?" asks a smart fox.
"I have a headache," says Leo.

Think!
Why didn't the fox trust the lion? Look and check your answers on page 120.

"You should **see a doctor**," says the fox.
"No," says Leo. "I don't like doctors."
"Then you should **take some medicine**," says the fox.
"No," says Leo. "I don't like medicine. I want you to help me. Come closer! Please look at my head."
"OK," says the fox. "But first, you should close your eyes. Sometimes, sunlight can hurt your head." Then she quietly **puts on a bandage**. The bandage is around Leo's ankles.
Leo opens his eyes. It's time to catch the fox. But he can't move!
The fox opens the bag. The parrot and the monkey jump out.
"Stop!" yells Leo. "That's my breakfast and that's my lunch!"
"Thank you!" say the parrot and the monkey.
"It's OK. But remember … you shouldn't trust a hungry lion!" says the fox.

3 Read again and write.

1. What's Leo like? Leo is lazy and smart.
2. Why does he have a stomachache? ____________________
3. Which animals does Leo put in his bag? ____________________
4. Who helps the parrot and the monkey? ____________________

4 Vocabulary Write the correct verbs. Then match.

1. ___see___ a doctor
2. ____________ in bed
3. ____________ some medicine
4. ____________ on a bandage

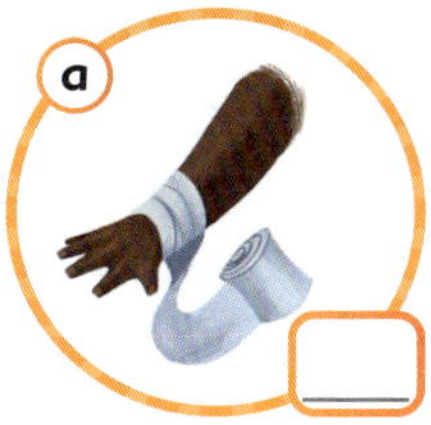

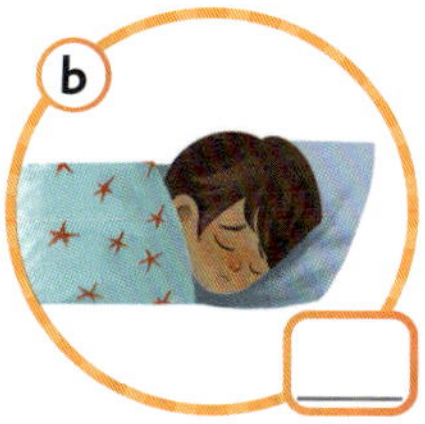

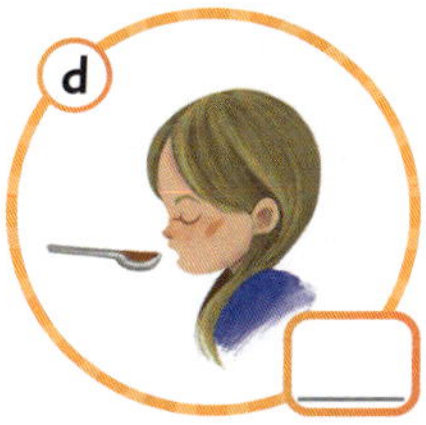

5 Discuss with a friend.

Following advice

1. Whose advice does the lion follow?
2. What advice does the fox give to the parrot and the monkey?
3. Do you think it's good or bad advice?

Responsible decision-making

I can read a fable about giving and following advice.

Language focus

1 (2.5) Listen and read. What's the matter with Flo?

Hi, Flo. Are you OK? You weren't in class today.

Hi, Ash. I feel sick. I have a headache.

Oh, no! That's too bad. You should take some medicine.

Thanks, Ash – that's good advice. I have a sore throat and a cold, too.

Did you see the doctor?

No, I didn't. My dad is taking care of me.

So, I guess you aren't going to basketball practice tonight?

No, I'm going to stay home and watch a movie.

You should stay in bed and get some rest. You shouldn't go to school tomorrow.

Thanks, Ash. Have fun at basketball practice!

2 Read again and check (✓) the good advice.

1 Flo should go to school. ◯
2 She should put on a bandage. ◯
3 She should take some medicine. ◯
4 She shouldn't go to basketball practice. ◯

3 Read, think, and say with a friend. Find similar sentences in the dialog.

Grammar Heroes page 120

should / shouldn't		
I You He / She We / They	should shouldn't	see a doctor. stay in bed. take some medicine. put on a bandage. play outside. go to basketball practice.

Speak up!

4 (2.6) Listen and repeat. Circle /s/ and underline /sh/.

1 I feel sick and my shoulder hurts.
2 You should see a doctor.
3 Samira shouldn't put on a bandage.

5 Imagine you are sick. Circle. Then ask and answer.

Health Survey

Do you …	
have a stomachache?	Yes / No
have a headache?	Yes / No
have a sore throat?	Yes / No
have a cold?	Yes / No
feel dizzy?	Yes / No
feel sick?	Yes / No

Health advice:
0 Yes answers = You feel good. You should go to school.
1–2 Yes answers = You should stay in bed.
3–8 Yes answers = You should see a doctor.

I can give advice for health problems.

Extra Lesson

Go online Phonics

Following advice

1 What examples of good and bad advice are there in the unit?

2 Listen and read. Then answer.

1 Which two texts say similar things?
2 Which texts match what you know about healthy food?

Reflect
Why is it important to follow the right health advice?

a

...

CHOCO-COOKIES

Our high-energy cookies are GREAT for young soccer stars!

The chocolate and sugar in these cookies give you a lot of energy.
You can eat them before and after a game.
Buy a big pack – you can share them with friends!

b

www.healthy.gov

Healthy Food for Sports

By Doctor Foster

"We should all eat healthy food."

Food before sports

Playing sports after a big meal can give you a stomachache.
Instead, have a healthy snack before you play.
Ask your doctor for more advice on healthy foods.

Food for energy

Carbohydrates give your body energy.
Some good carbohydrates are:

- rice
- whole wheat bread
- pasta
- fruit

Food for strong muscles

Protein helps your muscles grow.
You should eat some protein with every meal.

c

www.greenwooodschoolsoccerclub.edu

GREENWOOD SCHOOL SOCCER CLUB

Healthy Food Guide – by Mrs. Bones, Sports Teacher

Healthy food helps your body grow and gives you energy for soccer!

A healthy meal includes:

- a lot of fruit and vegetables
- a lot of good carbohydrates
- some proteins
- some dairy
- a little fat

3 Write a,b,c. Which text...

1 is from a doctor? b
2 wants to sell something? ____
3 is an education (.edu) website? ____
4 is a government (.gov) website? ____
5 gives different advice? ____

4 Choose one or two. Create a checklist to help find information you can trust.

1 Chocolate makes you happier.

2 All fast food is bad for you.

- Where can you go for advice?
- What should you look for on a website?
- Who should you listen to?

Useful Language
We can/can't trust this because ...
We shouldn't believe the information here.

LESSON 7
My world
Science

Healthy brains and routines

1 Read, listen, and answer.

2.8

1 How many hours should you sleep every night?
2 How many minutes should you exercise every day?
3 How much water should you drink?

Reading strategy

If you know the answer to a question is a number, scan the text quickly to find any numbers in it. For example, the numbers *9* and *10* refer to the number of hours you should sleep.

2 Vocabulary Read and complete.

It's important to have a healthy 1 ___routine___ . You should drink 2 ______ water. You should get enough 3 ______ at night. You shouldn't have too much 4 ______ . You should eat a good 5 ______ with lots of carbohydrates so your body has enough 6 ______ .

3 Which of these things can you change to make your brain more healthy?

food · exercise · sleep · water · air pollution · screen time

Disney In the real world

Rapunzel lives in a tower, but she tries to do a lot of different activities. This means she has a healthy body and brain.

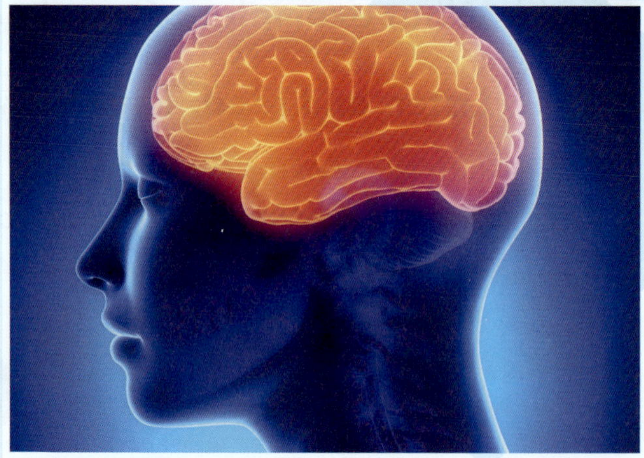

How can you have a healthy brain?

Your brain can ...
- think
- remember
- move your muscles
- help you communicate

Sleep

When you sleep, your brain remembers what happened that day. This helps you learn.

It's important to get **enough sleep** every night. Children should sleep between 9 and 10 hours a day. You shouldn't have **screen time** before you go to bed. It prevents you from sleeping well. You should read a book!

Food

Your brain needs energy to work. It gets energy from a sugar called **glucose**. Don't eat candy to get glucose – eat a **good diet**. We get glucose from healthy carbohydrates like pasta, rice, and fruit. You should always eat breakfast, lunch, and dinner so that your brain has enough energy.

I can read and understand about the brain.

Exercise

Your brain needs oxygen. When you exercise, your heart pumps blood and oxygen around your body to your brain. Your brain uses oxygen to turn glucose into energy.

You should exercise for 30 minutes or more every day. After you exercise, your brain can remember more new information. A **healthy routine** helps you have a healthy body and it makes you smart!

Water

Water takes oxygen to your body and your brain. When you don't drink **enough water**, you can feel dizzy and tired and have a headache.

Your brain is smart! It checks how much water there is in your blood. It makes you feel thirsty so that you want a drink.

You should drink about 6 to 8 glasses of water every day.

Your brain is awesome!

1 2.9 **Listen and circle what Ash should change. Say why.**

exercise   morning routine   diet

screen time   sleep   water

2 2.10 **Listen again and complete.**

Listening strategy
Read the timetable first to find out what kind of information is missing.

Ash's Routine

8:00 a.m.	drink ___water___
________	go to school
12:30 p.m.	eat ________ food
4:30 p.m.	________
________	eat dinner
7:30 p.m.	have ________

MINI-PROJECT

3 **Design a healthy routine.**

THINK Do you have a healthy routine? Discuss with a friend what you should change.

PLAN Design a healthy routine. Remember to think about brain health.
Workbook page 24

SHARE Present your routine to another group.

I can design a healthy routine.

LESSON 9
Writing project

An advice column

1 Read and write.

1 Who wrote to Nurse Isa?

____

2 What is their problem?

____

3 Who wrote the reply and why?

____

2 Read again. Find and underline in the text.

1 two **health problems**
2 two **pieces of advice**
3 two **time expressions**

Writing focus

In advice columns we can use set time phrases:

every morning	*when*
always	*before / after*

Ask the school nurse!

Dear Nurse Isa,

Every morning at school, I have a stomachache and I feel tired. Then I make a lot of mistakes. After lunch, I feel good again and my work is better. What should I do?

Ash, age 11

Dear Ash,

Do you eat breakfast every day? You should always eat a healthy diet. For example fruit, yogurt, and bread. It's important to drink enough water, too. You should go to bed early. You shouldn't have screen time before bed.

Nurse Isa

Let's write!

3 Write an advice column.

Think Think of a health problem. Think of reasons why it happens.

Get ready Work with a partner to think of three pieces of advice you can give for your problem.

You should get more sleep.

Problem: I can't get enough sleep at night.

Why?
↓
I'm not tired.
↓
Exercise outdoors.
Don't have screen time before bed.

Now exchange your problems with another pair/group.

Can they give more advice for your problem?

Can you give them advice for their problem?

Is the advice good advice?

Tip

Collaboration: group problem solving

By asking others for advice, you can come up with more creative solutions for your problem. Listen respectfully before choosing the ideas you think are best.

Plan and write Bring your best ideas together and write your advice column. **Workbook** page 25

I can write an advice column.

You can do it!

1 Match and write *should* or *shouldn't*. Then listen and check.

2.11

1 I have a headache.
2 I have a cold.
3 My shoulder and my elbow hurt.
4 I have a toothache.
5 I have a sore throat.

a You ______________ play outside.
b You ______________ play tennis.
c You should take some medicine.
d You ______________ drink a glass of warm milk.
e You ______________ eat candy.

2 Put the words in order to make sentences. Then write advice.

1 hurts / My / wrist — My wrist hurts. — You shouldn't write.
2 sleep / enough / I / get / don't ______________ ______________
3 have / stomachache / a / I ______________ ______________
4 always / I / dizzy / feel ______________ ______________
5 don't / water / enough / drink / I ______________ ______________

Let's talk! How can we stay healthy?

3 Tell a friend how you can stay healthy.

at home
at school
in your free time
with your diet

Movie quiz

1 When does Rapunzel see lights in the sky?
2 What happens when Rapunzel sings a special song?

I can ...

- use words related to health and body ☐
- talk about illness and give advice ☐
- identify information I can trust ☐
- write an advice column ☐

I completed Unit 2!

Go online
Big Project

3 Technology for the future

How can technology help us?

Look, think, and wonder.

1. What can you see?
2. What things in the pictures can you see in your classroom?
3. How is the house in the picture similar or different to your house?

1 (3.1) **Match the words to the pictures. Then listen, check, and repeat.**

→ Name three things that can be part of a laptop.

Vocabulary

1 remote
2 button
3 eco-home
4 scanner
5 touch screen
6 microphone

I can use technology words.

INCREDIBLES 2

Storyboard

2 3A **Watch the video and answer.**

Making good choices

1. Why should Dash stop using the remote?
2. How are Edna's costumes good for the environment?
3. "*You have powers!*" Are superpowers good, bad, or both?

Responsible decision-making

3 3.2 **Listen and write.**

Dash loves technology. He finds a **1** remote. He pushes a **2** ________ . Now there's a couch in the **3** ________ !

His baby brother, Jack-Jack, likes technology, too. At Edna's house, he touches the **4** ________ . He looks into the **5** ________ . He talks into the **6** ________ . Then the door opens. Jack-Jack thinks Edna's house is fun!

4 **What technology do you use in your home?**

I use a microphone and a remote.

LESSON 2

Vocabulary

technology

at home: TV

both: laptop

at school: whiteboard

1 Where do we use technology?

2 Read and listen. Then match.

3.3

There's an awesome new store in town. I'd like a new microphone.

...

Technology Megastore

Video Games

We have awesome 1 **game consoles** and 2 **wireless controllers**. Or why not put on a 3 **VR headset** and go inside your video game?

Drones

All our 4 **drones** have cameras and a touch screen remote. They're quiet and can fly quickly.

AI Speakers

5 **AI speakers** can answer your questions! They have microphones and they can play music and the radio, too.

Toys

Our 6 **robotic dog** toys are cute. They can walk and talk.
Our new 7 **hoverboard** is the fastest way to travel. You should try it.
Make your own toy with a 8 **3D printer**!

Come to our store ***today!***

a you use them to play video games [1] [ ]

b you can wear it [ ]

c it plays music [ ]

d they can move [ ] [ ] [ ]

e it makes things [ ]

3 Read again and write for you.

The best technology is the ____________ and ____________ .

The worst technology is the ____________ and ____________ .

4 What would you like to buy? Talk with a friend.

Talk buddies

Give your opinion by saying:

I agree.

I disagree.

I'm not sure.

What would you like from the store?

I'd like the 3D printer because it's the most modern.

I can use words for technology.

INCREDIBLES 2

1 Watch, read, and write *T* (true) or *F* (false).

1. There's a hovertrain at the station. ___T___
2. A hovertrain is slower than a normal train. ______
3. More people will travel by public transportation. ______
4. The people are travelling by hoverbus. ______
5. We will ride electric motorcycles. ______

2 Watch again. Check (✓) the sentences that are about the future.

1. It's a hovertrain and it's very fast. ◯
2. People will travel by public transportation. ◯
3. People drive cars every day. ◯
4. We won't travel by Elasticycle. ◯

3 Read, think, and say with a friend.

Grammar Heroes page 121

***will* for future predictions**		
Will	we	have robotic teachers? travel by hovertrain?
Yes, we will.		No, we won't.
We	will won't	ride electric motorcycles. use AI speakers in school. drive electric cars.

4 Ask and answer with a friend.

- have robotic pets
- use VR headsets at school
- live in eco-homes
- watch TV
- use game consoles

Will we live in eco-homes?

Yes, we will.

5 Write about the future. Share your ideas with a friend.

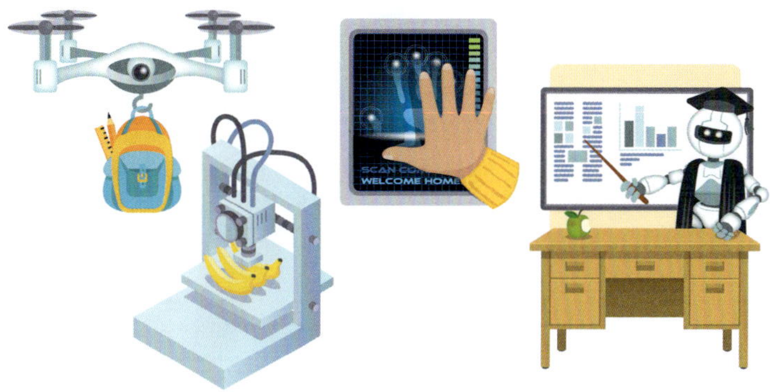

We will use 3D printers to make food.

The gift

1 Look at the story and answer.

1 Is the story set in the past, present, or future?
2 What is the surprise gift?
3 What looks better at the end of the story?

2 3.4 Listen and read. What two gifts does Grandma offer to Rafa?

Rafa loves his VR headset. He uses it to explore jungles in **virtual** worlds. He's sad because in the **real** world, there aren't any trees or plants. There are only gray skyscrapers and noisy highways.

Rafa gets a **hologram** call from his grandma. "I want to give you a gift." she says, "Would you like a robotic dog or a surprise? I can tell you one thing about the surprise – it's good for the environment."
"Can I please have the surprise gift?"
"Good choice." says Grandma.

Later, a drone arrives with the gift from Grandma. What will be inside the box?
Rafa and his mom look inside.
"I remember those," Mom says. "They are seeds."
"How do I grow seeds?" Rafa asks his AI speaker. "Seeds need soil, water, and sunlight to grow."

Think!

What seeds will Grandma send Rafa next? Look and check your answers on page 121.

Where can they find soil? Mom lifts up the **artificial** grass in the yard – there's soil under it! Rafa plants the seeds. He uses his drone to water them. Mom thinks there won't be any plants because the soil is bad.

After a few weeks, small green leaves begin to grow. They grow into beautiful plants, flowers, and trees. Now there are colorful insects and birds in his backyard. It's more beautiful than the worlds Rafa sees in his VR headset.

"Soon, there will be real strawberries on the plants," says Rafa. Will they taste better than artificial strawberries?

The strawberries are red now and they taste amazing! Rafa shares seeds with his neighbors and soon the neighborhood is green and colorful. He sends Grandma a hologram of their amazing backyard. "It's the best present in the world! Thank you!"

3 Read again and write.

1 What does Rafa explore with his VR headset?
He explores jungles.

2 What do seeds need to grow?
____

3 What do the seeds grow into?
____

4 What does Rafa give to his neighbors?
____

4 Vocabulary Write the correct words. Then match.

1 Plastic grass is artificial .
2 ____________ strawberries grow on plants.
3 We see ____________ worlds in video games.
4 A ____________ is a 3D picture.

a  ___

b 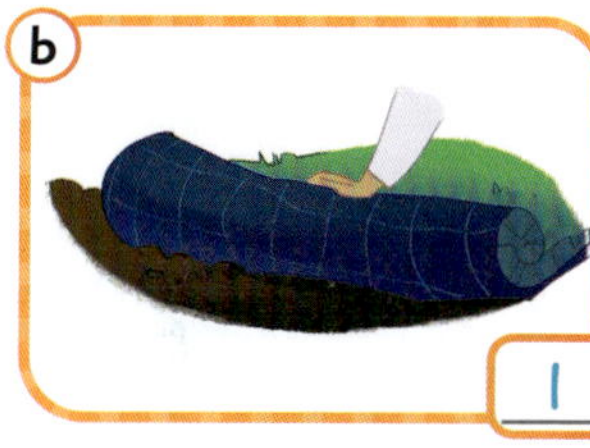 1

c  ___

d  ___

5 Discuss with a friend.

Making good choices

1 Why does Grandma say "*Good choice*" when Rafa chooses the surprise gift?
2 Why does Rafa decide to share his seeds?
3 How does the neighborhood change?

Responsible decision-making

I can read a science fiction story about making good choices.

LESSON 5

Language focus

1 Listen and read. What are Flo and Pablo talking about? (3.5)

Yesterday, I watched *Incredibles 2*. There's a lot of technology in the movie. Will we really have all that technology in the future?

I think so! What will teachers be like in the future?

I think there will be hologram teachers.

Cool! What will school lunch be like?

I think there will be artificial food. Maybe there'll be food made by a 3D printer!

Yuck!

What do you think school will be like?

I think there will be virtual schools. There won't be real schools. We'll use VR headsets at home.

Oh, no! Virtual schools will be lonely!

2 Read again and write *P* (Pablo) or *F* (Flo).

1 There won't be real teachers. P

2 There will be artificial food. _____

3 There will be virtual schools. _____

4 There won't be real schools. _____

3 Read, think, and say with a friend. Find similar sentences in the dialog.

Grammar Heroes page 121

will for future predictions			
What	will	schools teachers	be like?
There	will won't	be	artificial food. wireless schools.

Speak up!

4 Listen and repeat. Circle the word with the correct stress. (3.6)

1 There will be **hoverboards** / **hoverboards**.

2 There won't be **skateboards** / **skateboards**.

3 There won't be **microphones** / **microphones**.

5 Write your ideas about towns in the future. Then ask and answer.

Transportation
hovertrains

Homes
apartment blocks

Stores

Restaurants

What will homes be like in the future?

There won't be houses. There will be large apartment blocks.

I can make predictions about the future.

Extra Lesson

Go online Phonics

Making good choices

1 When do characters in the unit make good choices?

2 Listen and read. Complete the flow chart. 3.7

Choices | Cons (✗) | ~~Identify the problem~~ | Make a decision | Pros (✓)

How to make good choices

1 Identify the problem
My laptop touch screen doesn't work.

2 ____________

I can fix it.

Pros (✓)
It will be less expensive than a new laptop.
It will be better for the environment.

Cons (✗)
It will take time to fix it.
It will be difficult.

I can buy a new laptop.

3 ____________
I will have a new laptop quickly.
I can recycle my old laptop.

4 ____________
It will be expensive.
It will be worse for the environment.

5 ____________
I will fix the touch screen.

Useful Language
The pros / cons are …
This is better / worse for the environment.

3 Create a flow chart for the problem below and make a decision.

I joined a swimming club. How can I get to the pool? → **Choices:** on foot, by bike, by car …
→ **Pros:** cheap, good exercise, …
→ **Cons:** hard work, not good if the weather is bad, …

4 Reflect on your decision with a friend.

Is it good for the environment?

Is this the best decision?

Are there better choices?

Reflect
Why is it important to make good choices for the environment?

Responsible decision-making I can make good choices.

LESSON 7
My world

Technology 3.8

Eco-technologies

1 Read, listen, and answer.

1 Why do people choose to live in eco-homes?
2 What are underground homes like in summer?
3 Name two technologies that use AI.

Reading strategy
Labels on pictures and diagrams can explain new vocabulary or ideas quickly.

2 Vocabulary Read and match.

1 A composting toilet
2 Solar panels
3 Wind turbines
4 Smart fridges and ovens
5 Water tanks
6 Bioplastics

a get energy from the wind.
b get energy from the sun.
c doesn't use water.
d collect water.
e are made from plants.
f use AI.

3 Which technologies help with waste? Which help with energy?

smart oven · wind turbine · solar panels · composting toilet · water tank

Disney In the real world

Elastigirl is happy. She chooses an electric motorcycle because it's good for the environment.

Eco-homes

What will eco-homes be like in the future?

Most homes use a lot of energy to keep them warm or cool. Some people think we'll build more homes underground in the future. The temperature of underground homes only changes a little. They are cool in summer and warm in winter. This is good for the environment because underground houses use less energy.

People can grow their own food on the roof of an underground home. It's also better for wild animals and insects.

Today, we can get energy from **solar panels** on roofs. Solar panels use sunlight to make energy. In the future, we'll have solar panel technology in windows, too.

In a lot of countries, finding water is a problem. Eco-friendly homes could have **water tanks** to collect rainwater.

I can read and understand about eco-technologies.

Some homes will have **wind turbines** too, to get energy from the wind.

What will it be like inside an eco-home?

A **smart fridge** uses AI. It can tell you what food you should eat and what you should buy. Smart ovens cook food more quickly. Smart technology will help us waste less food and use less energy.

In the future, we'll use **bioplastic** trash bags. Bioplastic is made of plants so it biodegrades better than normal plastic.

Some people think meat is bad for the environment. In the future, we will eat more artificial meat made of plants.

Many toilets waste a lot of water. Eco-homes will have **composting toilets** that don't use water.

Technology in eco-homes *will* protect the environment!

1 3.9 **Listen and circle the two things they are getting at the school today.**

wind turbine   water tank
smart fridge   solar panels

2 3.10 **Listen again and complete.**

Listening strategy
Look at the words before and after the gaps.
Are they part of a compound noun?
solar + panel = compound noun

bioplastics   smart   ~~solar~~   tank

Summerhill School: Eco-school plans

Today, we're getting **1** ___solar___ panels on the roof.

2 ________ technology will record how much energy we make and use.

We're getting a bigger water **3** ________ so that we can collect rainwater and water the plants around the school.

In the cafeteria, we want to reduce waste. We also want to use more **4** ________ in the kitchen.

MINI-PROJECT

3 **Design eco-technology for your school.**

THINK How's your school good/bad for the environment? Discuss with a friend.

PLAN Choose one of the problems and think of ideas to help.
Workbook page 36

SHARE Present your eco-technology invention to another group.

A descriptive text

1 Read and write.

1 Is this Flo's real bedroom?

____

2 What kind of things does she label?

____

2 Read again and write.

caption label title

1 robotic cat ______________

2 A scanner will open the door. ______________

3 My futuristic bedroom ______________

Writing focus

A descriptive text is about one thing: a person, place, object or event. Each section has a main topic. You can use bullet points to list more specific details.

My futuristic bedroom

by Flo

There will be an AI speaker in my bedroom. It will:

- play music
- change the color of the lights
- help me with my learning

There won't be a television, a game console, or wireless controllers. There will be a VR headset with a microphone.
I will use the VR headset to:

- play computer games
- talk to my friends
- watch movies

Let's write!

3 Write a descriptive text.

Think Think about what bedrooms will be like in the future.

bed windows desk music technology

I think we'll have smart beds!

Get ready Work with a partner to answer the questions in the diagram.

Plan and write Create your futuristic bedroom with labels and captions. **Workbook** page 37

Present Present your descriptive text to the class.

Tip

Presentation: using visuals and digital tools

Use colors, labels, arrows, etc to show which part of your picture you are talking about. Use digital tools to animate your bedroom design and reveal bullet points one at a time.

What's the title?
- Amal's awesome bedroom in 2050

What's in the picture?
- 3D printer
- game console
- wind turbine on roof
- bed with remote

What are the captions?
- All the technology is wireless.
- The 3D printer makes toys.

What are the labels?
- wind turbine
- remote

I can write and present a descriptive text.

You can do it!

1 Listen and write.

1 Will people use remotes? No, they won't.
2 Will I play with a wireless controller? ____________________
3 Will we use 3D scanners to make toys? ____________________
4 Will you have a robotic pet? ____________________
5 Will children go to a real school in the future? ____________________

2 Write questions and answers.

1 (countryside) What will the countryside be like? There will be artificial trees.
2 (teachers) ________________________________ There won't be real teachers.
3 (cars) ________________________________ There will be hovercars.
4 What will homes be like? (eco-homes) ____________________
5 What will technology be like? (smart technology) ____________________

Let's talk! How can technology help us?

3 Tell a friend some ways technology can help the environment.

at home
communication
transportation
at school

Movie quiz

1 Who stays home to look after the kids?
2 Who makes the superhero costumes?

I can ...

- use words related to technology and eco-homes ☐
- make predictions about the future ☐
- make good choices ☐
- write a descriptive text ☐

I completed Unit 3!

Go online
Big Project

4 Curious and creative!

What things can we create?

Look, think, and wonder.

1. What can you see?
2. Which clothes do you like?
3. Which clothes do you think are the most creative?

1 4.1 **Match the words to the pictures. Then listen, check, and repeat.**

→ Which words describe patterns?

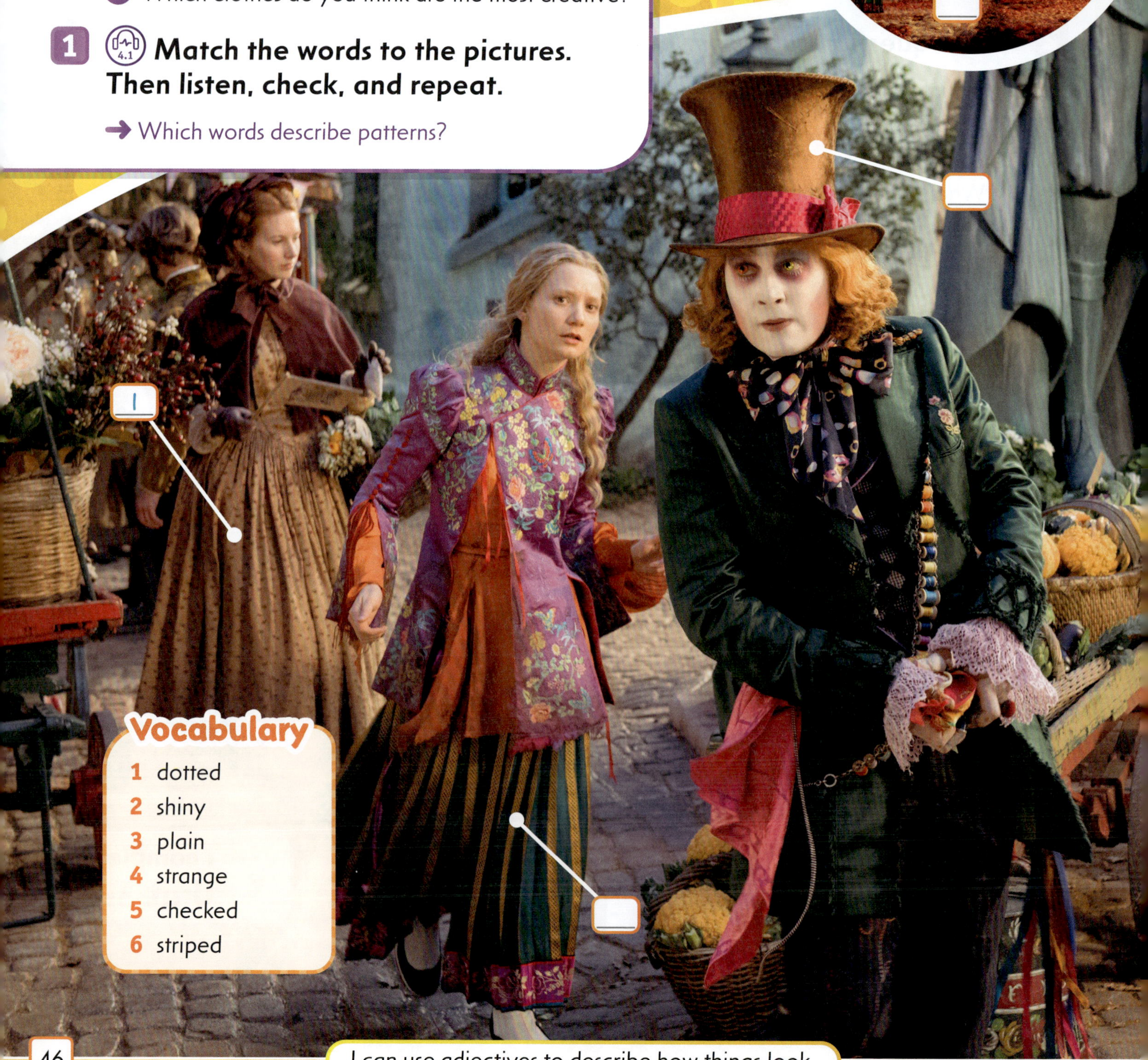

Vocabulary

1 dotted
2 shiny
3 plain
4 strange
5 checked
6 striped

I can use adjectives to describe how things look.

Disney ALICE THROUGH THE LOOKING GLASS

Storyboard

2 Watch the video and answer.

Appreciating creativity

1. How is Alice different from other people?
2. How is The Mad Hatter creative?
3. *"Anything is possible!"* What is unusual about Underland?

Social awareness

3 Listen and write.

Concept art

Alice doesn't like 1 ___plain___ clothes. She's wearing a colorful 2 ___________ skirt from China. The Mad Hatter is Alice's friend. He lives in Underland. He's wearing a dark green coat. It's 3 ___________ . The Mad Hatter makes 4 ___________ hats. His hat has a pink, 5 ___________ ribbon on it. Will he make Alice a 6 ___________ hat, or a striped hat?

4 Describe what you are wearing.

I'm wearing a striped shirt and shiny shoes.

LESSON 2
Vocabulary

size	color	pattern	look
tiny	light	dotted	strange
	pink		modern

1 What adjectives do you know?

2 4.3 Read and listen. Then match.

ASH'S BE CREATIVE BLOG

Unusual Food Market Taste Test →

This week I tried four new, unusual foods. Some were delicious, some were strange, and some were horrible!

This week on my creative blog, I'm focusing on unusual food. Check out these ideas.

1 Olive ice cream ....

I love ice cream and I love **olives**, but this was horrible!

2 Coffee yogurt ....

This was OK, but **coffee** in yogurt was strange. It tasted a bit like lemons. It was a little sour.

3 Honey burger ....

I loved this burger! The **honey** sauce was shiny and delicious.

4 Sugar mice ....

The **sugar** mice were cute and colorful, but they were also very sweet.

Join me next week when I'm going to look at creative clothes.

a It was **sour**. [2]

b It was **delicious**. [___]

c They were **sweet**. [___]

d It was **horrible**. [___]

3 Imagine and write for you.

I tried a coffee and chocolate cake.

It was sweet and delicious!

I tried ______________________ .

It was ______________________ .

4 Describe an unusual food to a friend.

Talk buddies

Ask your friend to give reasons for their views:

Why didn't you like it?

Why was it (horrible)?

I tried a pizza with pineapple and olives on it.

What was it like?

It was horrible!

I can use words related to food.

Disney ALICE THROUGH THE LOOKING GLASS

1 Watch, read, and circle.

Mirana took a tart from the kitchen and ate it. It **1 looked** / **sounded** delicious. It **2 felt** / **smelled** like strawberries. It **3 looked** / **tasted** sweet. Her mother asked "Where is the tart?" Mirana didn't tell the truth. Iracebeth was sad and angry. She ran out of the palace. She fell and hit her head. Now her head **4 looks** / **smells** big.

2 Watch again. Read and write.

modern shiny soft ~~sour~~ creative

1. The tart doesn't taste ____sour____ .
2. The Red Queen's dress looks ________ and ________ .
3. The White Queen's dress looks ________ .
4. The White Queen's voice sounds ________ .

3 Read, think, and say with a friend.

Grammar Heroes page 122

Describing something		
What does it	look / sound / feel / smell / taste	like?
It	feels smells tastes looks sounds	hard. horrible. delicious. like a heart. like a bird.

4 Ask and answer with a friend.

What does it look like?

It looks like a flower.

It's the hat!

Yes!

1

2

3

4

5 Describe something in your classroom to a friend.

It looks small. It smells sweet.
It tastes like fruit. It's my snack.

I can describe things.

Charlie's creative cakes

1 Look at the story and answer.

1 What kind of food is in the story?
2 What do you think the king is like?
3 Is this fiction or non-fiction?

2 Listen and read. What do they eat at the picnic?

Many years ago, in the Kingdom of Battenburg, there was a lazy, mean king. King Kucher liked eating cake, but he didn't like sharing. One day, he said to the people, "You aren't important enough to eat cake. All cakes are for me. You can eat bread." The people thought the king was horrible.

King Kucher ate delicious cake for breakfast, lunch, and dinner. He ate too much cake. Every day, the people worked hard and ate their bread. They forgot what cake tasted like.

Charlie lived with his parents. They were bakers, and they baked bread. Charlie loved books. One day he said to his mother, "There aren't enough books in town. Please can I have a book for my birthday?" His mother found an old recipe book. "You can have this."

Charlie read recipes for delicious cakes: big cakes with shiny **frosting**, coffee cakes, sweet honey cakes, and sour lemon cakes.

He asked, "Can we make a cake?"

His father said, "It's too dangerous. The king's men put cake bakers in the castle."

Think!

What food do the cakes look like? Look and check your answers on page 122.

Charlie was smart. He said, "What if we make a cake, but it doesn't look like a cake?" Charlie and his parents put **butter**, **flour**, eggs, **spices**, milk, and sugar in a bowl. "That's enough sugar," explained his dad. "Don't put in too much."

The cake baked in the oven. It smelled delicious!

They put chocolate frosting on the cake.

"It looks like bread!" said Charlie.

The next day, the king's men looked at the bread in the baker's shop. They didn't see the cake.

Charlie didn't want to be like King Kucher, so he shared his recipes and ideas with his friends. Soon the town smelled like sugar and spices.

On Saturday, they all had a picnic in the countryside. At the town gate, the king's men looked in their bags and said, "It's just a picnic, there isn't any cake here!"

"This is the most creative picnic ever!" said Charlie, laughing.

3 Read again and write.

1. Who eats cake every day?
   The king eats cake every day.
2. Why is it dangerous to make cake?
   ____
3. What do the people do at the end?
   ____

4 Vocabulary Write the correct words to complete the recipe. Then match.

200g brown sugar
200g soft 1 butter
4 eggs
200g white 2 ________
2 tablespoons milk
some 3 ________
100 g chocolate 4 ________

a  \[\]

b 

\[\]

c  \[1 \]

d 

\[\]

5 Discuss with a friend.

Appreciating creativity

1. Where does Charlie find his ideas?
2. What makes the cake look like bread?
3. What do the people learn to make?

Social awareness

I can read a traditional story about being creative.

LESSON 5

Language focus

1 Listen and read. What ingredients are in the cookies?

4.5

Look at the boat cookies I made for my Be Creative blog.

They look delicious, but there aren't enough sails.

I didn't have enough paper.

Do they taste good?

Hmm… there are too many spices in the cookies. And there isn't enough frosting. I want to make some more, but there isn't enough sugar or butter.

Well, I like the frosting.

There are too many cookies for my family – do you want some?

Yes, please! 😊 I want to be creative like you!

You can be creative! Why don't you make something for my next blog?

2 Read again and write *T* (true) or *F* (false).

1 There aren't enough spices in the cookies. F

2 There's too much frosting. ____

3 There isn't enough sugar. ____

4 There are too many cookies for Ash's family. ____

3 Read, think, and say with a friend. Find similar sentences in the dialog.

Grammar Heroes page 122

Quantifiers		
There's	too much	frosting.
There isn't	enough	paper.
There are	too many	sails.
There aren't	enough	colors.

speak up!

4 Listen and repeat. Draw arrows when the nouns go up and down.

4.6

1 There aren't enough **paints**, **pencils**, and **markers**.

2 There isn't enough **coffee**, **sugar**, and **honey**.

3 There are too many **olives**, **spices**, and **mushrooms**.

4 There's too much **paper**, **wool**, and **glue**.

5 Look and read. Do you have what you need to make a banner?

You need:

1 x checked paper

2 x dotted paper

2 x striped paper

3 x plain paper

There's too much checked paper.

I can describe quantity.

Extra Lesson

Go online Phonics

Appreciating creativity

1 How do characters in the unit show creativity?

2 Listen and look at the notes. Then look at the diagram and write *a*, *b*, or *c*.

Creative people:
1 Ask questions like why, how, and what if?
2 Aren't afraid to make mistakes.
3 Use what they know already.
4 Share ideas.
5 Solve problems.
6 Try new things.

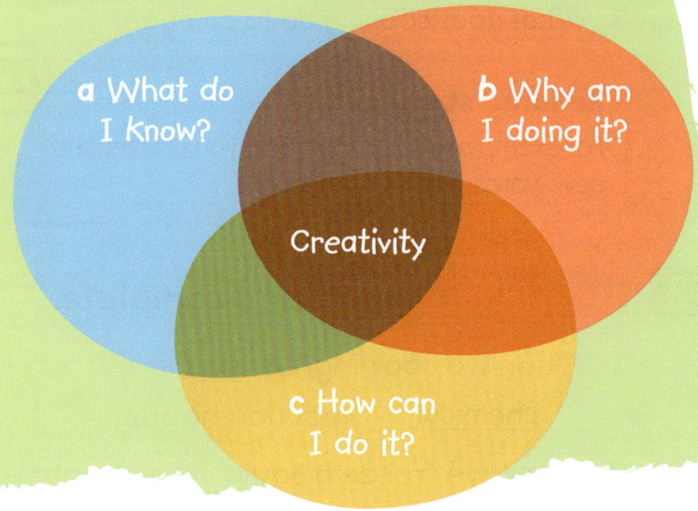

1 I want to make an unusual present for my mom. _____
2 I know she likes striped things and drinking coffee. _____
3 I can buy a plain cup and paint stripes on it. _____

3 Choose a picture and answer with a friend.

What questions did the creator ask?

What skills do they have?

What new things did they try and why?

1 

2 

3 

4 

5 

4 Copy the M and create a picture. Then compare and discuss in your group.

- Which idea is the most creative?
- Did you have similar ideas?
- Which strategies from 2 did you use?

Useful Language
They aren't afraid to …
What if we …?
They know how to …

Reflect
When is it good to be creative?

Social awareness I can appreciate creativity.

LESSON 7
My world
Science

Chemistry and food

1 Read, listen, and answer.

4.8

1 Where does the energy come from to make a cake?
2 What happens when you melt chocolate?
3 What does cooking do to an egg?

Reading strategy
For example and *e.g.* can help you understand new words and ideas in a text.

2 Vocabulary Read and complete.

1 When we cook ingredients, a ___chemical___ reaction happens.
2 When we freeze a liquid, it turns into a ____________ .
3 Melting chocolate is a ____________ change.
4 Cooking eggs is an ____________ change.
5 The cold liquid becomes a ____________ when it touches the warm air.
6 Cooks can make ____________ into many different shapes.

3 Cooking food always causes irreversible changes. True or false?

DISNEY In the real world

In the film *Alice Through the Looking Glass*, the delicious tarts looked like flowers. Chemistry can make cooking even more creative.

Every time you cook a meal, it's science!

For example, we stir cake ingredients and cook them in an oven. The energy from the hot oven changes the ingredients into a cake. This is a chemical reaction. The cake looks, tastes, smells, and feels different from the ingredients.

Reversible and irreversible changes

We can change ingredients into other things by stirring, cooking, and freezing.

For example, we can stir and freeze ingredients to make ice cream. We can change a liquid into a solid by freezing it.

We can change a solid into a liquid by melting it. For example, we can melt cheese.

Some changes are **reversible**. When we melt chocolate, it changes from a **solid** to a **liquid**. When we cool the liquid chocolate, it changes from a liquid back to a solid.

Some changes are **irreversible**. When we cook an egg, it changes from a liquid to a solid. We can't change the cooked egg back to liquid – the change is irreversible.

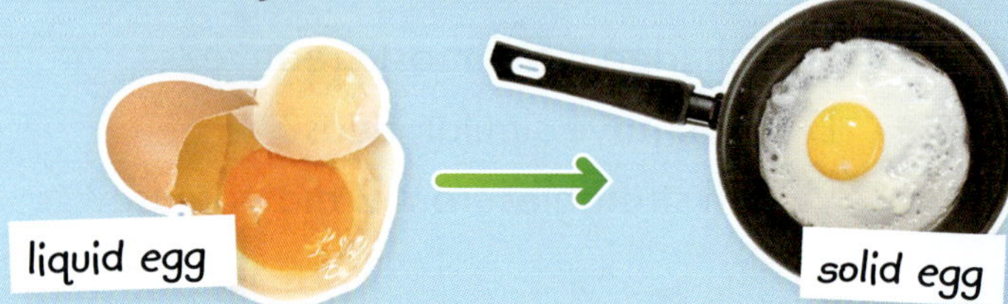

I can read and understand about food chemistry.

Creativity with chemistry

Modern cooks use science to create amazing foods. For example, they use a very cold liquid to freeze ingredients quickly. It's a quick way to make ice cream and it looks amazing! The liquid freezes the cream and at the same time, it becomes **gas** when it touches the warm air.

A **gel** is strange because it is both a liquid and a solid. It's solid on the outside, but liquid on the inside. It can taste like fruit, meat, vegetables, or fish. Cooks can be creative with gels because they can make them into any shape. They can look like a ball, a cube, or even a pyramid.

1 (4.9) **Listen. Where did Ash eat lunch?**

Listening strategy
The first time you listen, try to get a general idea. Don't worry about details.

2 (4.10) **Listen again and complete.**

Menu

We use 1 ___chemical___ reactions to make exciting food. Our ingredients are delicious and unusual.

Carrot plant
Noodles with 2 ______________ , olive soil, and carrots.

Honey and fruit 3 ______________
Delicious balls of strawberry, honey, and mango.

Quick freeze ice cream
From liquid to 4 ______________ in seconds in a cloud of 5 ______________ .

MINI-PROJECT

3 **Invent a creative meal.**

THINK What unusual meals do you know?

PLAN Invent and write notes for your meal.

Workbook page 48

SHARE Present your meal to the class.

I can invent a creative meal.

A blog post

1 Read and write.

1 Who wrote this blog?

____

2 What is the blog about?

____

2 Read again. Find and underline in Emily's blog.

1 a **heading**
2 an **introduction**
3 a **description** of the first candle
4 an **opinion** of the second candle

Writing focus
Adjectives always go in this order:
quantity + opinion + size + age + shape + color + noun
There are two horrible, large, new, round, purple gels.

10:02

Creative candles

March 20th

Hi! I'm Emily. I made some creative candles for Ash's blog.

First, I made a small, square, orange candle with lemons and coffee. There aren't enough lemons in the candle, and there is too much coffee. It smells horrible and I think it looks plain.

Next, I made a pretty, tall, striped candle. The orange stripe smells like honey. The green stripe smells like spices. It looks like a pyramid. The candle smells delicious, but I think there are too many colors.

Which candle do you like?

Let's write!

3 Write a blog post.

Think Think of or imagine an item you have made. What was it like?

food | fashion | crafts

I made a scarf. It was soft, colorful and woollen.

Get ready Work with a partner to answer these questions:

What's the heading for your blog? | How can you describe your item? | What's your opinion of your item?

Plan and write Analyze the task and write your blog post. **Workbook** page 49

Tip
Self-management: analyzing the task
Make sure you understand the writing task. Make a list or map of the different sections you need to include in your blog, then add more detail to the sections.

Heading
↓
Introduction
↓
Description
↓
Opinion

I can write a blog post.

YOU CAN DO IT!

Test your progress with English Benchmark Young Learners

1 Listen and write. (4.11)

1 There's ____too____ ____much____ frosting.
2 There ________ ________ spices.
3 There ________ ________ butter.
4 There are ________ ________ olives.
5 There's ________ ________ coffee.

2 Read and match. Then write.

1 What does the frosting look like?
2 What does sugar look like?
3 What does a lemon taste like?
4 What does flour feel like?
5 What does honey smell like?

a It ________ soft.
b It ________ like salt.
c It ________ sweet.
d It ________ sour.
e It ____looks____ delicious.

Let's talk!

What things can we create?

3 Tell a friend how you were creative this week.

clothes music sports cooking

Movie quiz

1 What kind of insect is Absolem?
2 How many queens are there?

I can ...

- use words to describe things, food and clothes ☐
- describe things and talk about quantity ☐
- appreciate creativity ☐
- write a blog post ☐

I completed Unit 4!

Go online
Big Project

5 Carnival fun

Why is it important to have fun?

Look, think, and wonder.

1. What can you do at a carnival?
2. Would you like to go to this carnival?
3. Which ride looks the most exciting to you?

1 (5.1) **Match the words to the pictures. Then listen, check, and repeat.**

→ Name two rides that go in a circle.

Vocabulary

1. carnival
2. rides
3. Ferris wheel
4. rollercoaster
5. carousel
6. bumper cars

I can use carnival words.

Disney · PIXAR TOY STORY 4

Storyboard

2 Watch the video and answer.

5A

Knowing what we value

1. *"There's only one Forky!"* Why is Forky special to Bonnie?
2. Which character values their freedom?
3. At the end, who is the most important person in Woody's life?

Self-awareness

3 Listen and write.

5.2

Woody and Bo explore a 1 carnival. There are a lot of 2 ______________ and stalls there. The 3 ______________ looks fun, but the 4 ______________ looks scary! Younger children love the 5 ______________. The 6 ______________ are exciting, but they're noisy, too. Will Woody and Bo go on a ride?

4 Imagine. What will you do at the carnival?

I'll go with my best friend. We'll go on the carousel.

1 What activities can you do at a carnival?

go on ...	eat ...	drink ...	watch ...
the bumper cars	candy	milkshakes	a parade

2 Read and listen. Then match. (5.3)

CARNIVAL DAYS

We're going to the carnival for my birthday on Saturday. I'm so excited!

Come to the carnival today! 1 **Go to the entrance** near the park. You can 2 **buy a ticket** at this entrance. You can 3 **wait in line** at the entrance from 10.00 a.m.

Are you ready for fun?

4 **Take your seat** in our new Rocket Rollercoaster. You'll love it!

Are you hungry or thirsty?

You can 5 **bring a snack** and you can 6 **bring a water bottle** from home. Or visit one of our food and drink stalls.

Families

Remember to 7 **stay together**. Lost children should 8 **go to the exit** where they can meet their families.

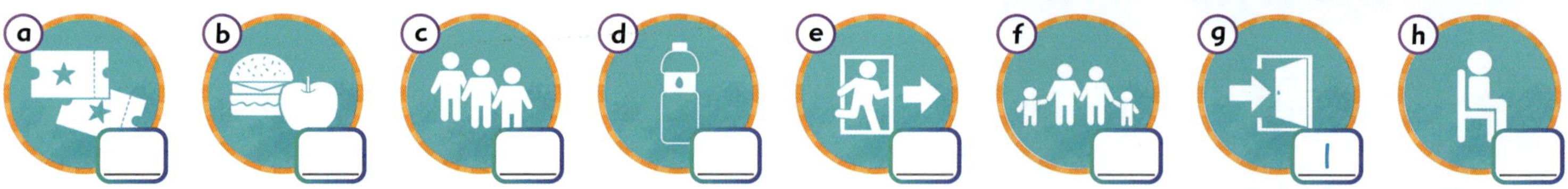

3 Write for you.

At the carnival, I can ______________________.

At the carnival, I should ______________________.

4 Plan a day at the carnival. Talk with a friend.

We should buy tickets for the rides first. What do you think?

Sure, then we can go on the bumper cars.

Talk buddies

Check your plans by asking:
Is that OK with you?
What do you think?
What else do you want to do?
What next?

I can use words for carnival activities.

Disney · PIXAR TOY STORY 4

1 Watch, read, and write.

1. Woody wants to explore the carnival .
2. There's a carousel, a Ferris wheel, and ________ .
3. You have to buy a ________ to go on a ride.
4. The children have to wait in ________ .
5. Woody and his friends have to stay ________ .

2 Watch again. Read and write *T* (True) or *F* (False).

1. Woody has to go with the other toys. F
2. Woody and Bo don't have to buy a ticket for the rides. ____
3. The children don't have to wait in line. ____
4. The girl doesn't have to hit the planet. ____
5. The man has to buy more prizes. ____

3 Read, think, and say with a friend.

Grammar Heroes page 123

have to / don't have to		
You / We	have to	wait in line.
	don't have to	buy a ticket.
She / He	has to	stay together.
	doesn't have to	go to the entrance.

4 Say and guess with a friend.

CARNIVAL **LIBRARY**

be quiet
buy a ticket
bring a water bottle
bring a snack
use a computer

You don't have to use a computer.

It's the carnival!

5 Write rules for a movie theater. Share your ideas with a friend.

You have to take your seat.
You ...

I can talk about what people have to do.

A DAY AT THE CARNIVAL

1 **Look at the story and answer.**

1 Is this a biography, a play, or fiction?
2 How do the boy and girl know each other?
3 Do the characters enjoy the carnival?

2 5.4 **Listen and read. Does Jordan want to take Talia to the carnival?**

At breakfast, Talia said, "The carnival is in town! Please can we go, Mom?"
"I'm sorry," said Mom. "I have to work today. Jordan can take you."
Talia loved hanging out with her big brother, but Jordan had other ideas.
"I don't want to go to the carnival with her," said Jordan. "I want to **hang out** with my friends." Jordan's free time with his friends was important to him.
"Jordan, I have to work, so you have to take Talia to the carnival," said Mom.

"Look, a carousel!" said Talia at the carnival. "Oh and that stall **sells cotton candy**. Can I have some?" But Jordan was very grumpy. "I'm not interested in going on rides with you, and I'm not going to buy you cotton candy!" Talia was sad because she wanted to be with her brother.

Then she saw a poster for her favorite show. Talia was excited about it.
"Please can we **see the show**? I want to see Gray Wing – he's my favorite!"

"Hey, Jordan! We're waiting in line to **go on the ghost train**." It was Jordan's friends. Jordan said to Talia, "You have to stay here and wait for me,"
Talia didn't want to wait alone for him, "We have to stay together!" But he didn't listen.

On the ghost train, Jordan was scared. There were scary monsters and lots of scary noises. He was worried about Talia.

Think!
What's Mom's job? Look and check your answers on page 123.

Jordan met Talia after the ride finished. "I'm sorry, Talia," said Jordan. "Let's see the show now."

"We're too late!" said Talia.

"Wait here," said Jordan. He went behind the theater. Suddenly, Gray Wing jumped out and said, "Hello, Talia! I have some cotton candy for you!"
Talia was excited about Gray Wing.
Then his helmet fell off. It was Jordan!
Jordan's friends said, "That was awesome, Jordan. You're a cool brother!"
Talia, Jordan, and his friends went on the rides together.
Time with family and friends is the best!

3 Read again and write.

1 Why can't Mom go to the carnival? She has to work.
2 Does Jordan go on the carousel? ______
3 Why doesn't Jordan like the ghost train? ______
4 What does Jordan wear at the end of the story? ______

4 Vocabulary Write the correct verbs. Then match.

1 I want to ___go___ on the ghost train.
2 The stall ______ cotton candy.
3 It's fun to ______ out with our friends.
4 Do you want to ______ a show?

a  [ ]

b  [1]

c  [ ]

d  [ ]

5 Discuss with a friend.

Knowing what we value

1 Who does Talia want to hang out with?
2 At the beginning, does Jordan value time with family or friends more? Why?
3 What does Jordan learn at the end?

Self-awareness

I can read a contemporary fiction story about knowing what we value.

LESSON 5
Language focus

1 Listen and read. What do they decide to do together?

Hey Ash, do you want to hang out at the carnival on Saturday?

I have to ask Mom and Dad. They're worried about me going alone.

It's OK. My parents are coming. I'm excited about the rollercoaster.

But you have to wait in line for 45 minutes. That's boring.

True. Let's decide on Saturday.

OK. I'm interested in seeing the show. And eating cotton candy!

Yes, me too. Oh, and we have to go on the ghost train!

No way! I'm scared of ghosts!

Oh, Ash! Ghosts aren't real!

2 Read again and write.

1 What are Ash's parents worried about?
Ash going to the carnival alone.

2 What's the problem with the rollercoaster?

3 What's Ash interested in?

4 What's Ash scared of?

3 Read, think, and say with a friend. Find similar sentences in the dialog.

Grammar Heroes page 123

Adjectives and prepositions		
He's	worried about scared of	the bumper cars. horror movies.
What	are you is she	excited about? interested in?

Speak up!

4 Listen and repeat. Underline the silent letters.

1 I'm excited about the **ghost** train.
2 I'm scared of the **Ferris wheel**.
3 I'm interested in your **answer**.
4 I'm worried about my **knee**.

5 Complete the survey for you. Then ask and answer.

My feelings survey

	Me	My friend
worried about	exams	
interested in	dinosaurs	
scared of		
excited about		

What are you worried about?

I'm worried about my exams.

I can talk about how I feel about things.

Extra Lesson

Go online Phonics

Knowing what we value

1 What things do characters in the unit value?

2 Listen, read, and do. Then answer.

5.7

1 Should we all value the same things?
2 Does what we value change?

What do you value?

We value things that are important to us like our hobbies, our things, and our family and friends. We can also value things like being honest, nice, creative, and polite. Different people value different things. You can use these questions to understand your values and how they play a part in your life. This will help you learn more about who you are.

Step 1: Identify when you were very happy or proud.

- What were you doing?
- Where were you?
- Who were you with?
- Why did you feel happy or proud?

Step 2: Identify the things you value most.

List what you value and then decide which things are the most important. Think about these things:

family | friends | hobbies | being healthy | sports | teamwork | being popular | my things | creativity | learning

Step 3: Reflect.

What you value most will change over time. For example, today you value being at school with your friends. In 10 years, maybe you will value traveling to new countries. But some values will stay with you for life.

Reflect
Why do people value different things?

3 Make a Values Tree. Write your ideas on the leaves.

4 Reflect on your values with a friend.

I'm more interested in being creative than being sporty.

Useful Language
I value … more than …
I'm more interested in … than …
The most important thing to me is …

Self-awareness I can recognize and understand what I value.

Rollercoasters

1 Read, listen, and answer. (5.8)

1 Which force pulls things to the center of the Earth?
2 Which force slows the rollercoaster down?
3 What stops the rollercoaster at the end of the tracks?

Reading strategy
Look at the whole sentence to help you guess the meaning of a difficult word.

2 Vocabulary Read and complete.

A rollercoaster moves on 1 ___tracks___ . At the 2 ____________ , a force called 3 ____________ quickly pulls it down towards the Earth. Many rollercoasters have fun 4 ____________ you go around. At the end of the ride, 5 ____________ use the force of 6 ____________ to slow the rollercoaster down.

3 Which of these things use brakes? Can you think of any others?

bike | hot air balloon | car | plane | train | scooter | boat

How do rollercoasters work?

Most rollercoasters don't have an engine and they don't use fuel. Rollercoasters use a force called **gravity** to move.

Gravity

What happens when you jump in the air? Do you stay up in the air? No, you go back down again.

Things that go up come down again because gravity pulls things to Earth.

How does a rollercoaster use gravity?

1 At the start of the ride, a machine pulls the rollercoaster slowly up the **tracks**. Energy from the pull of gravity builds as the rollercoaster goes higher. The machine has to pull stronger than the pull of gravity.

2 At the **top**, the rollercoaster uses this energy to drive to the end of the tracks.

3 Then, gravity pulls the rollercoaster down. It gets faster and faster.

4 Now the track climbs up again. This time, gravity pushes down on the rollercoaster. But the rollercoaster has enough energy to get to the top again.

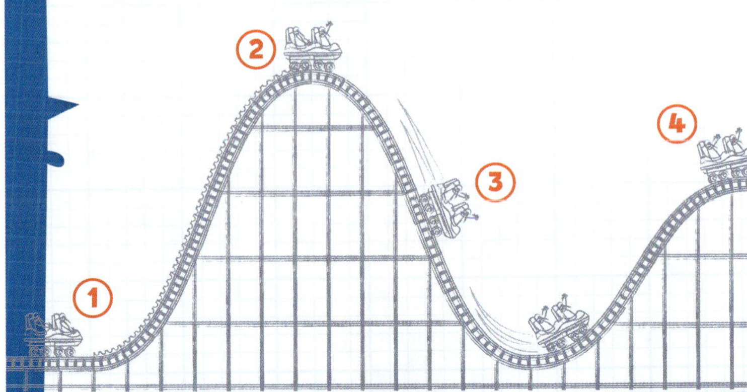

Disney In the real world

Buzz goes on rides at the carnival. But how do rides work?

I can read and understand how rollercoasters work.

Are you interested in rollercoasters? READ ON!

Loops

1 Energy pushes the rollercoaster slowly up the **loop**. It climbs up.

2 At the top, gravity pulls it down again quickly.

Rollercoasters are fun because they go slowly then quickly, and they go up and down.

How does a rollercoaster use friction?

Rollercoasters use another force to slow down. This force is called **friction**. Friction is a force between two surfaces that slide across each other. The rollercoaster slides along the tracks. We don't want much friction for the rollercoaster to go fast, but we need friction to make it stop.

The rollercoaster has to stop at the end of the track. It uses **brakes** to stop. The brakes create more friction between the rollercoaster and the tracks.

1 5.9 **Listen. What did Emily win?**

Listening strategy

Listen to how people are talking. How do you think they feel about the topic?

2 5.10 **Listen again and circle.**

Summerhill News

A fantastic new waterslide opens today. Emily designed it and she was the first to try it. The waterslide has five exciting **1 tracks / loops**. You move very quickly because there isn't much **2 friction / gravity**. The waterslide is very high, so **3 gravity / friction** pulls you down quickly. Emily is **4 worried / interested** in engineering. She wants to design carnival rides in the future. Good luck, Emily!

MINI-PROJECT

3 **Design a marble rollercoaster.**

THINK In groups, discuss what is important in your design.

gravity loops friction

PLAN Complete your first design.
Workbook page 60

SHARE Present your design to the class.

I can design a marble rollercoaster.

LESSON 9
Writing project

An invitation

1 Read and write.

1 Who's the writer?

____

2 What's the invitation for?

____

3 Where are they going?

____

4 Is it in the morning or afternoon?

____

Celebrate my birthday with me!

Where: The carnival.

When: Saturday May 21st.
Meet at the entrance at 2:00 p.m.

Other information: Bring a water bottle, but you don't have to bring a snack. Mom and Dad are going to buy snacks there.

Please reply to my mom and dad by this Friday.
They have to buy the tickets this weekend.

From,
Emily

Rides: We're going to go on the Ferris wheel first. I'm excited about it!

Show: There's a show next to the carousel. We have to take our seats at 3:15 p.m. We can meet the performers after the show.

2 Read again. Check (✓) the information in the text.

1 the date ◯
2 the time ◯
3 phone number ◯
4 what to bring ◯
5 school name ◯
6 the place ◯
7 where to meet ◯
8 age ◯

Writing focus

Names of places, days, months and people's names begin with a capital letter.
You should write the month first, then the date, then the year.
Use a.m. (morning) or p.m. (afternoon).

Let's write!

3 Plan and write an invitation for a carnival trip.

Think What do you want to do at the carnival? Think of your top three activities.

I'd like to see a show.

I really want to go on the rollercoaster.

Get ready Work in a group to answer these questions.

Where and when will you meet?
The carnival entrance Friday 14th April at 4.00 p.m.

What will you do?
ghost train, bumper cars

What other information will your guests need?
Bring a snack.

Plan and write Write your invitation as a group. **Workbook** page 61

Tip

Collaboration: sharing responsibilities

Plan your event as a group, with each person taking responsibility for a different part of the invitation, e.g. time, activities. This way everyone contributes equally!

I can write an invitation.

You can do it!

1 Write. Then listen and match. (5.11)

1 ✓ She ___has___ to — d
2 ✗ They ______ to
3 ✓ You ______ to
4 ✓ We ______ to
5 ✗ He ______ to

a wait in line for the rides.
b stay together at the carnival.
c go on the ghost train.
d buy a ticket for the carousel.
e go to the exit behind the Ferris wheel.

2 Put the words in order to make questions. Then write the answers.

1 excited / What / you / about? / are — *What are you excited about?*
(bumper cars) — *I'm excited about the bumper cars.*
2 you / worried / What / are / about? ______
(ghost train) ______
3 in? / you / are / interested / What ______
(the show) ______
4 of? / are / you / What / scared ______
(rollercoaster) ______

Let's talk! Why is it important to have fun?

3 Tell a friend which of your values you can enjoy at a carnival.

family friends my things fun

Movie quiz

1 Which old friend does Woody meet in the store?
2 How is Forky different from the other toys?

I can ...

- use words related to a carnival ☐
- talk about what people have to do ☐
- recognize and understand what I value ☐
- write an invitation ☐

I completed Unit 5!

Go online Big Project

6 Let's solve it!

How can we encourage each other?

Look, think, and wonder.

1. Describe the characters.
2. What are the characters interested in?
3. What mystery stories do you know?

1 6.1 **Match the words to the pictures. Then listen, check, and repeat.**

→ What else do detectives usually have?

Vocabulary

1 magnifying glass
2 fingerprint
3 notebook
4 footprint
5 badge
6 detective

I can use words about solving mysteries.

Disney · PIXAR ONWARD

Storyboard

2 Watch the video and answer. (6A)

Encouraging others

1. What are Ian and Barley trying to do?
2. Who does Ian encourage at the restaurant?
3. "*You can do this.*" Who encourages Ian at the bridge?

Relationship skills

3 Listen and write. (6.2)

Colt isn't a 1 detective, he's a police officer. He wears a police 2 ____________ on his shirt. He works at the police station. He sometimes uses a 3 ____________ to make clues look bigger. You can use it to look at 4 ____________ . Detectives also look for 5 ____________ in mud or paint. They write notes in their 6 ____________ . Colt is looking for Ian and Barley. Will he find them?

4 **You're going to solve a mystery. What will you take with you?**

I'll take a notebook and a pencil.

1 What mystery words do you know?

2 Read and listen. Then match.

6.3

THE MYSTERY CHANNEL

I love mysteries! What's on the Mystery Channel tonight?

6:00 Detective Danni

Danni has always wanted to be a detective. Danni has to 1 **solve a mystery** at the library. Watch Danni 2 **investigate the crime**. Will she 3 **follow the clues** and find the stolen books?

6:30 History Mysteries

The team 4 **make a discovery** in Italy. Watch them use magnifying glasses to look at Ancient Roman footprints.

7:00 Crime News

Every day, we 5 **gather information** about local crimes. We also 6 **interview witnesses**. 7 **Watch the news** and find out what's new today.

7:30 Sixty Seconds

Can you do the puzzle in 60 seconds? This puzzle show is for you! 8 **Crack the codes** and win a prize!

a
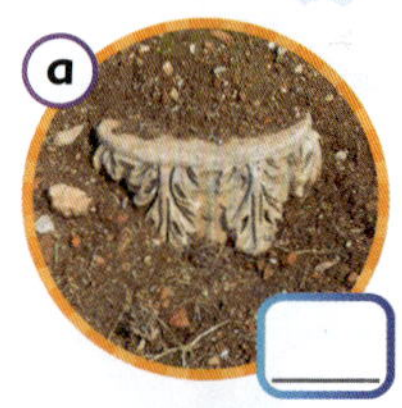

b

c

d

3 Write for you.

I want to gather information about the world.

I want to ______________________

______________________.

I don't want to ______________________

______________________.

4 What do you want to watch? Talk with a friend.

Talk buddies

Give your friend feedback by saying:

That sounds interesting / boring / cool / exciting.

We should watch History Mysteries.

It's about Ancient Rome. They make a discovery in Italy.

Why?

That sounds interesting.

I can use phrases related to investigations.

Disney · PIXAR ONWARD

1 Watch, read, and circle.

1. Mom had to gather **fingerprints** / **information** quickly.
2. The detective was **interviewing** / **watching** the Manticore.
3. Ian and Barley were following **clues** / **footprints**.

2 Watch again. Read and match.

1. What was Ian doing on his birthday? c
2. What was Barley doing in the afternoon? ___
3. What were Barley and Ian doing in the evening? ___
4. What was Mom doing in the evening? ___

a. He was trying to solve the mystery.
b. She was looking for her boys.
c. He was looking at his notebook.
d. They were gathering information.

3 Read, think, and say with a friend.

Grammar Heroes page 124

Past Progressive				
What	were	you / they	doing	at 9:30 a.m. / p.m. ? on Monday? in the morning?
	was	he / she		
They	were	solving a mystery. gathering information. looking at a notebook.		
I / He / She	was			

4 Ask and answer with a friend.

3 p.m.

watch the news

4 p.m.

investigate a crime

4:30 p.m.

follow clues

5 p.m.

make a discovery

What was the detective doing at 3 p.m.?

She was watching the news.

5 Write questions. Then ask a friend and write their answers.

What were you doing at 9 a.m. on Saturday?

I can ask and answer about past activities.

MYSTERY AT THE MUSEUM

1 Look at the story and answer.

1 Is this fiction or non-fiction? What tells you?
2 Where is the story set?
3 Is the story set in the present, past, or future?

2 6.4 Listen and read. Who took the necklace?

Detective Tarek Watson was reading the newspaper. "Listen to this, Eliza: *Bad News at the Museum. Police ask: Where is the Ancient Roman necklace?*"

They had to investigate the crime! But then Tarek fell and hurt his foot.

At the hospital, the doctor said, "You have to stay in bed."
Tarek said, "You have to solve the museum mystery alone, Eliza."
Eliza said, "I can't! I'm not a detective, I'm an **assistant**!"
"You're really smart. You can do it," said Tarek.

Eliza interviewed the museum **security guard**.
"Were you working last night?"
"Yes, I was." He answered. "The doors were closed. I didn't see or hear anything."

Then, Eliza interviewed the **manager**.
"Were you working here last night?" she asked.
"No, I wasn't. I was reading a book at home," she said. "Those birds are noisy!" She closed the window.
Eliza used her magnifying glass. There weren't any footprints or fingerprints. "Was the **cleaner** working last night?" Eliza asked the manager.
"No, he wasn't, but he's working now."
The cleaner was grumpy, "There aren't any clues, but there's a lot of trash! There's even a feather on the floor!"
Eliza looked at the feather with her magnifying glass. How did it get there?

Think!

What else did the thief take? Look and check your answers on page 124.

Eliza was thinking about the clues when a bird flew up into a tree. Eliza had an idea! She climbed up the tree and looked into the nest. She found the necklace!

Eliza and Tarek visited the museum. Tarek said, "Good job, Eliza. You solved the museum mystery. Here, you should have a detective badge, too!"

3 Read again and write.

1 Why can't Tarek investigate the crime? He's at the hospital.
2 What was the security guard doing last night? ______
3 What was the manager doing last night? ______
4 Where did Eliza find the necklace? ______

4 Vocabulary Write the correct jobs. Then match.

1 I take care of the museum. I'm a security guard .
2 I clean the museum. I'm a ______ .
3 I work in the office. I'm a ______ .
4 I help the detective. I'm an ______ .

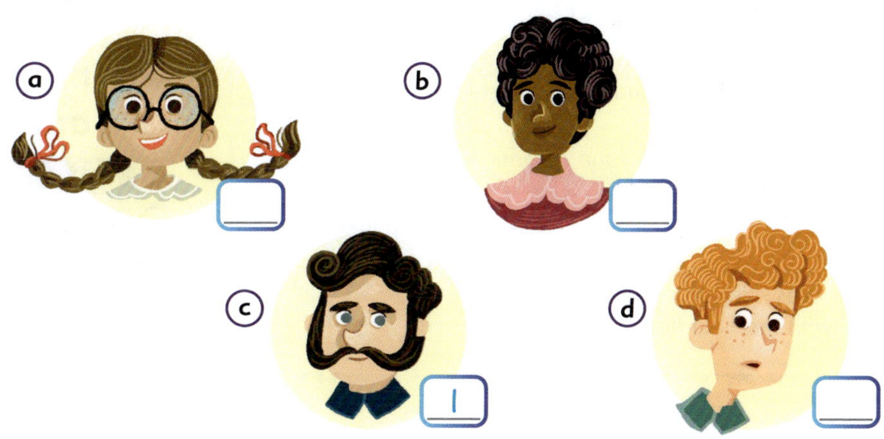

5 Discuss with a friend.

Encouraging others

1 Why does Eliza think she can't solve the mystery?
2 Who encourages Eliza?
3 What encouraging messages does he use?

Relationship skills

1 Listen and read. What jobs are mentioned?

6.5

Hi, Flo. Were you watching the Mystery Channel yesterday?

No, I wasn't. I was helping my aunt. She's the manager of an escape room. I was her assistant for the day.

What's an escape room?

It's a game. Your team has one hour to solve mysteries before the door opens. Look.

Cool. 😊 Were you solving the mysteries?

No, I wasn't. I was interviewing the teams. I was gathering information about their visit.

Were you interviewing teams all day?

Yes, I was. I helped Victor the cleaner, too.

Was your uncle there?

Yes, he was. He's the security guard. Come with me next time!

2 Read again and write *was* or *wasn't*.

1. Flo wasn't watching TV yesterday.
2. She _______ helping her aunt yesterday.
3. She _______ solving mysteries yesterday.
4. She _______ interviewing teams yesterday.

3 Read, think, and say with a friend. Find similar sentences in the dialog.

Grammar Heroes page 124

Past Progressive – questions and short answers			
Was	she	watching TV? cracking codes?	Yes, she was. No, she wasn't.
Were	they	interviewing teams? following clues?	Yes, they were. No, they weren't.

Speak up!

4 Listen and repeat. Circle /f/ and underline /v/.

6.6

1. Was the detective following footprints?
2. Was Philip solving a mystery?
3. Was Fred interviewing Stephanie?
4. Were the friends taking photos?

5 Play a guessing game. Ask and answer.

Were you whistling a tune?

Yes, I was.

You're number 6!

I can ask and answer about past activities.

Extra Lesson

Go online Phonics

Encouraging others

1 How do characters in the unit encourage each other?

2 6.7 Listen and check (✓) the phrases you hear. Which phrases are helpful?

1 Sure, you can. ☐
3 I believe in you. ☐
5 You figured it out! ☐
2 Hurry up! ☐
4 You almost did it. ☐
6 No! Let me do it. ☐

3 Work in groups of three to solve a mystery.

Useful Language
You'll get better at it.
Try again.
Let's work together.
You figured it out!

Oh, no! The gold trophy is missing from the swimming pool.

You are the detectives. Work in teams to solve the mystery.

1 In your group, take turns to do the roles for each puzzle.
Manager: watch the time!
Code-cracker: solve the puzzle
Cheerleader: encourage the code-cracker

2 Solve the puzzles in order. You have three minutes.

1 When did the crime happen?

2 What were they doing when the crime happened?

Crack the code!

1	2	3	4	5	6	7	8	9	10	11	12	13
A	B	C	D	E	F	G	H	I	J	K	L	M
14	15	16	17	18	19	20	21	22	23	24	25	26
N	O	P	Q	R	S	T	U	V	W	X	Y	Z

1 The manager was 23 15 18 11 9 14 7 working in his office.
2 The cleaner was 3 12 5 1 14 9 14 7 ____________ the showers.
3 The security guard was 23 1 20 3 8 9 14 7 ____________ the news.
4 The assistant was 5 1 20 9 14 7 ____________ in the café.

3 Who did it?

1st letter in **mystery** m
2nd letter in **badge** ___
3rd letter in **fingerprint** ___
2nd letter in **watch** ___
1st letter in **gather** ___
4th letter in **notebook** ___
2nd letter in **crack** ___
It was the ____________.

Remember! Encourage your team.

4 Reflect on how you solved the mystery.

Who was the best manager / code cracker / cheerleader?

Reflect
How do you feel when you encourage your team?

Relationship skills I can encourage others.

LESSON 7
My world
Art

Ancient art

1 Read, listen, and answer.

6.8

1 What did a builder find near the volcano?
2 What was inside the buildings?
3 Name three types of Ancient Roman art.

Reading strategy
Numbered lists help you follow instructions.

2 Vocabulary Read and circle.

1 An **engineer** / **artist** makes art.
2 A **historian** / **builder** studies the past.
3 A **fresco** / **mosaic** is a picture made from stone or glass.
4 A **fresco** / **sculpture** is a picture painted onto a wet wall.
5 You put **pictures** / **plaster** onto walls before you paint them.
6 A **mosaic** / **sculpture** is a work of art in 3D. It's often made from stone.

3 Compare Ancient art with Modern art. How are they similar? How are they different?

portraits, sculptures, jewellery, frescoes, mosaics, fountains, buildings

Disney **In the real world**

Barley is interested in history and making discoveries. Art historians make discoveries about the past, too.

ART MYSTERIES

In 79CE, a big cloud of stone and gas fell from a volcano.

More than 1,600 years later, a builder made an amazing discovery near the volcano. He found houses, stores, and roads underground. It was the ancient city of Pompeii.

Historians found beautiful Ancient Roman art inside the buildings.

Frescoes

Roman **artists** painted pictures onto walls. The pictures are called **frescoes**. They tell us a lot about how people dressed, what they ate, and about their hobbies and sports.

This fresco shows a group of people. Were they playing a game? Historians think they were.

How to make a fresco

1 Put wet **plaster** on the wall.
2 Mix your paint.
3 Paint your picture quickly, before the plaster dries!

Sculptures

Sculptures were popular, too. Many houses and stores in Pompeii had sculptures made from stone.

Some houses had beautiful fountains, too.

This is a sculpture of the emperor Marcus Aurelius.

I can read and understand about Ancient Roman

Mosaics

Some Romans had **mosaics** in their houses. They used small squares of glass or stone to make a pattern or a picture.

This mosaic shows there was a dog in the house.

This mosaic shows there was a fish store here.

How to make a mosaic

1 Cut glass or stone into small squares.
2 Put wet plaster on the wall or floor.
3 Stick the squares on the plaster to make a picture.

Art historians are making new discoveries in Pompeii every day. They find things from the past and investigate how old they are and what they are. Sometimes it takes years to gather information and solve the history mystery.

Now you solve it!

What do you think Ancient Romans used these things for?

1 6.9 **Listen. Who is Leo and what is he making?**

2 6.10 **Listen again and complete.**

~~artist~~ fresco mosaic plaster sculpture

Listening strategy

Read the text before you listen and predict the missing word. Then listen and check your predictions.

Leo's Art Club Home | News | Gallery

It's your turn to be an **1** ___artist___! Last week we were making a modern **2** ______________ from trash. This week, we're going to make a paper **3** ______________. It's easy, and you only need paper and glue! Have a go – you can do it!

Next week, we're going to make a **4** ______________. It's fun, but messy! You need to buy some **5** ______________ to make this.

MINI-PROJECT

3 **Make a piece of ancient art.**

THINK Research Ancient Roman mosaics. Choose one to copy.

PLAN Draw your design on squared paper and color it in.

Workbook page 72

SHARE Present your mosaic to the class.

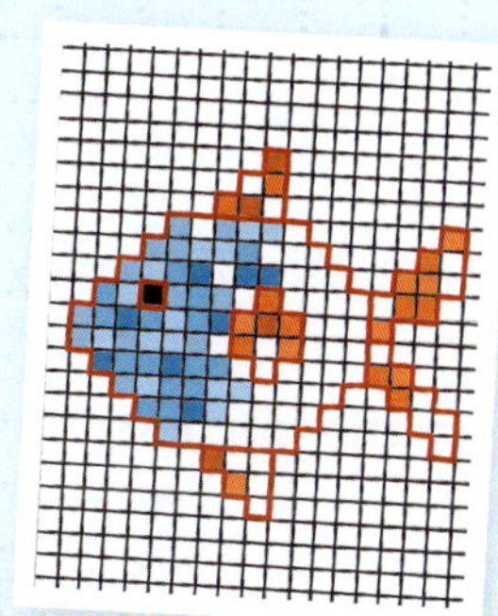

I can design a piece of ancient art.

A playscript

1 Read and write.

1 What's the title of the play? ______________________
2 Who are the characters? ______________________
3 Where does the scene take place? ______________________

The Mystery of the Queen's Crown

[In the Queen's bedroom.]

Tarek: *[worried]* We have to find the Queen's crown.

Eliza: *[confident]* We should gather information. Let's interview the Queen.

[The Queen enters]

Queen: *[worried]* I looked for my crown this morning at 11 o'clock but it wasn't in the box!

Tarek: What were you doing at 9 o'clock this morning?

Queen: I was horseback riding.

Eliza: Were you swimming at 10 o'clock?

Queen: No, I wasn't.

[Cleaner enters]

Cleaner: *[impatient]* I have to clean this room.

Tarek: We're investigating a crime!

Cleaner: And I'm cleaning. Look at these footprints.

[Eliza uses a magnifying glass]

Eliza: *[excited]* The footprints end at the wall.

Tarek: *[interested]* Look. There's a door painted on the wall.

2 Read again. Underline the words that tell you how the characters feel. Act out the playscript.

Writing focus

We use stage directions to tell actors:
- what to do *[enter room]*
- how to say lines *[excited]*

We use [ ] for stage directions.

Let's write!

3 Write a playscript.

Think What do you think happens next in the story? Share ideas.

What's behind the door?

I think there's a secret passage!

Tip

Presentation: bringing your play to life!

Plays are written to be performed! First, write your script, then rehearse in your group. Can you go back and improve your stage directions to make your play more exciting?

Get ready Work in a group to answer these questions.

Where is your play set? – in the garden

What props do you need? – a notebook, a magnifying glass

Who are the characters? – the Queen, the assistant, the detectives, the security guard

Plan and write Write your playscript. Workbook page 73

Present Present your playscript to the class.

I can write and present a playscript.

YOU CAN DO IT!

1 Listen, circle, and write. 6.11

1. Was the detective writing in his notebook? Yes / (No), he wasn't.
2. Were they making a discovery? Yes / No, ______________.
3. Were you using your magnifying glass? Yes / No, ______________.
4. Was she investigating a crime? Yes / No, ______________.
5. Was I wearing my badge? Yes / No, ______________.

2 Complete the questions. Then write the answers.

1. What were you doing at 9 a.m.?
   (follow clues) I was following clues.
2. What ______________ he doing at 3 p.m.?
   (interview a witness) ______________
3. What ______________ they doing at 11 a.m.?
   (gather information) ______________
4. What was she ______________ at 5 p.m.?
   (watch the news) ______________
5. What were we doing ______________ 2 p.m.?
   (crack a code) ______________

Let's talk! How can we encourage each other?

3 Tell a friend when you need encouragement.

playing sports rehearsing a play
doing a hobby learning a language

Movie quiz

1. How are Ian and Barley different?
2. Who do Ian and Barley need help from in order to solve the mystery?

I can ...

- use words related to mysteries ☐
- talk about what I was doing in the past ☐
- encourage others ☐
- write a playscript ☐

I completed Unit 6!

Go online
Big Project

7 Everyday life

What lessons do you learn in everyday life?

Look, think, and wonder.

1. What can you see?
2. What are the characters doing?
3. What do you think their life is like?

1 **Match the words to the pictures. Then listen, check and repeat.** (7.1)

→ Which words are places and which are everyday items?

Vocabulary

1. vase
2. hallway
3. music box
4. fireplace
5. chest of drawers
6. cottage

I can use words about household places and objects.

Storyboard

2 Watch the video and answer. (7A)

Accepting when I'm wrong

1. Why does the Beast change from a prince?
2. What does Belle think of the Beast at the start?
3. *"There's something in him ..."* What does Belle think of the Beast at the end?

Social awareness

3 Listen and write. (7.2)

Concept art

Belle and her father lived in a **1** cottage . There were flowers in a **2** ____________ on the **3** ____________ . One day, Maurice traveled to town to sell his **4** ____________ at the market. He saw a wolf and rode to a castle. He walked into the **5** ____________ . In the dining room, there was a fire in the **6** ____________ .

4 Describe your house.

We have a small hallway. There's a chest of drawers. It's made of wood.

1 What household chores do you know?

activity	item	room
wash	the dishes	kitchen
clean	the floor	bathroom
		bedroom

2 7.3 Read and listen. Then match. What does Ash still have to do?

Dear Ash,

While we are out, can you and your sister help around the house?

To do

Please can you:

- 1 **sweep the floor**
- *clean the hallway*
- 2 **dust** *the living room – remember to dust the music box!*
- 3 **buy groceries** *(milk, bread, apples)*
- 4 **clean upstairs** *and* **downstairs**
- 5 **do the laundry**
- 6 **garden** *(water the plants, cut some flowers and put them in a vase)*

And don't forget to 7 **study**! *You have a math test tomorrow!*

There's some cake in the kitchen for you both.

Thanks,

Mom & Dad

Mom and Dad need my help around the house. This is their to-do list.

Finished jobs ✓

a 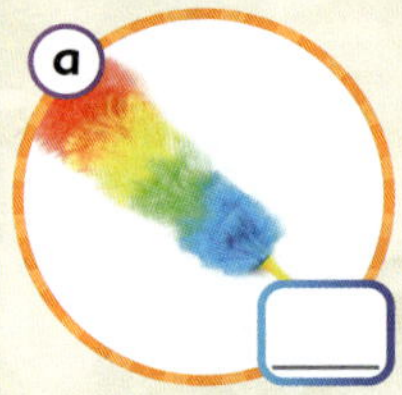 ___

b  ___

c  ___

d  1

e  ___

f  ___

3 Write for you.

How I help every day:

I have to ______________________ .

I don't have to __________________ .

4 What do you do around the house? Talk with a friend.

How often do you have to clean your bedroom?

Well, I have to clean my bedroom once a week.

Talk buddies

Give more information by saying:

Well, I have to … once a week.

Let's think …

I never ….

I can use words for household chores

Disney BEAUTY AND THE BEAST

1 Watch, read, and circle.

1. Belle walked into the village to buy **tickets** / **groceries**.
2. Belle was doing the **laundry** / **dishes** and reading.
3. The teacher said, "Girls shouldn't **study** / **dust**.
4. Belle followed Gaston into the **garden** / **hallway**.

2 Watch again. Read and match.

1. What was Belle doing when school started? ☐
2. What was she doing when the teacher yelled? ☐
3. What was she doing when she met Gaston? ☐

a. She was walking home when she met Gaston.
b. She was teaching a girl to read when the teacher yelled.
c. She was doing the laundry and reading when school started.

3 Read, think, and say with a friend.

Grammar Heroes page 125

Interrupted Past					
What	was	she / he	doing	when	the people arrived?
	were	you			the phone rang?
She / He	was	doing the laundry	when	the door opened.	
We	were	studying		the phone rang.	

4 Ask and guess with a friend.

1

2

3

4

What were you doing when the phone rang?

I was sweeping the floor when the phone rang.

Picture 2!

Yes!

5 Write questions. Then ask a friend and write their answers.

What were you doing when your mom came home?

I can ask and answer about interrupted events in the past.

MRS. KHAN'S MISTAKE

1 Look at the story and answer.

1 How does Mo help Mrs Khan?
2 How do you think the characters know each other?
3 How do you know this is a graphic comic?

2 7.4 Listen and read. How does the vase break?

Think!

Why does Mrs. Khan need help? Look and check your answers on page 125.

3 Read again and write.

1. Who takes Mrs. Khan to the market? Her daughter takes her to the market.
2. Who breaks the glass vase? ______________________________
3. Why does the bird go into the box? ______________________________
4. Why does Mrs. Khan give cake to Mo? ______________________________

4 Vocabulary Write the correct verbs. Then number in order.

a  ☐

A bird flew into the room, but it wanted to ____________ .

b  ☐

Mo decided to ____________ a box and put cake in it.

c 

☐

The bird made a glass vase ____________ the table and ____________ on the floor.

5 Discuss with a friend.

Accepting when I'm wrong

1. What does Mrs. Khan think of Mo at the start?
2. Why does Mrs. Khan yell at Mo when she comes home?
3. Why does Mrs. Khan say sorry to Mo at the end?

Social awareness

I can read a graphic comic about accepting when you're wrong.

1 Listen and read. Who's Fluffy?

7.5

Hi, Flo. I couldn't study for the science test yesterday. I had to go to the hospital.

Oh, no! Why did you go to the hospital?

I was cleaning downstairs when my cat, Fluffy, climbed onto the bookcase.

My sister wanted to tell Dad, but I was worried about Fluffy. I climbed onto the chest of drawers to rescue her. Then I fell off and broke my arm.

Poor you!

It's my fault. I'm sorry I didn't listen to my sister.

What happened to Fluffy?

Dad got some cat food to feed Fluffy. She climbed down to get it!

2 Read again and match.

1 Ash couldn't study for
2 Ash climbed onto the chest of drawers
3 Dad got some cat food
4 Fluffy climbed down

a to rescue Fluffy. [ ]
b to get the food. [ ]
c to feed Fluffy. [ ]
d his science test. [1]

3 Read, think, and say with a friend. Find similar sentences in the dialog.

Grammar Heroes page 125

Infinitives of purpose		
Why did	he / she	go to the hospital? make a cake?
He / she	went to the hospital made a cake	to see the doctor. to surprise a friend.

Speak up!

4 Listen and repeat. Draw ↗ for questions that go up at the end or ↘ for questions that go down at the end.

7.6

1 Did you buy groceries? ↗
2 Why did you buy groceries?
3 Did you clean the kitchen?
4 Why did you clean the kitchen?

5 What did you do on the weekend? Write notes. Then ask and answer.

I cooked a meal — to help my parents — to practice cooking

I went to the mall — to buy some jeans — to hang out with my friends — to see a movie

What did you do on the weekend?

I cooked a meal to help my parents.

I can ask and answer about purpose in the past.

Extra Lesson

Go online Phonics

Accepting when I'm wrong

1 When do characters in the unit learn that they were wrong?

2 7.7 Look at part a. Listen, read, and answer. Repeat for part b.

a

Shen's diary

I worked with Mike in class today. I was talking to him when he fell asleep! I had to work alone because he was too tired. Mike doesn't study enough. I think he's so lazy. I don't want him as a partner.

b

I said to Mike, "I think you're playing computer games at night. You are lazy." Mike looked sad.

Then our teacher said, "Mike has some happy news! Tell us about your new baby sister."

Mike said, "She's cute, but she cries a lot at night. In the evenings, I help my parents clean the house and do the laundry."

1 What do you think Mike is like?
2 Why do you think he fell asleep in class?

3 Now what do you think Mike is like?
Why do you think Mike fell asleep in class?

3 Look. Then read and circle.

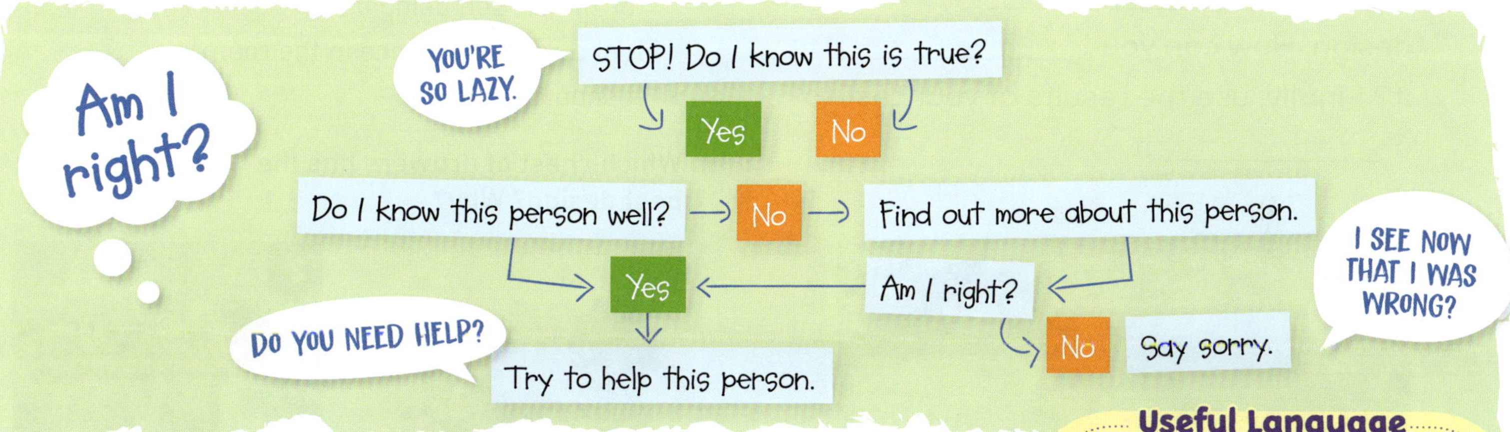

1 Did Shen know Mike was lazy? **Yes / No**
2 Did Shen know Mike well? **Yes / No**
3 Was Shen right? **Yes / No**
4 What should Shen do? **Help Mike change / Say sorry**

Useful Language

I thought …,
but I was wrong.
The truth was different.
I should have checked the facts.

4 Read and reflect. Then discuss with a friend.

When did you last say sorry because you were wrong about someone?

Why were you wrong?

How did you figure out you were wrong?

Reflect

How can you say sorry when you're wrong about something?

LESSON 7
My world
Technology

The design process

1 Read, listen, and answer.

7.8

1 What's the first design question?
2 How many stages are there?
3 What four things does the text say you can use to make your model?

Reading strategy
Headings tell you what a paragraph is about.

2 Vocabulary Read and complete.

First, identify the 1 ___purpose___ of your design. Next, decide which 2 ____________ you will use. Then make a 3 ____________ of your design. Now, 4 ____________ your design. How can you 5 ____________ it? Finally, use the results of your test to 6 ____________ it.

3 Which is more important – how something looks or what it does?

Disney In the real world

Maurice designs and makes music boxes. They play music and they look beautiful, too.

THE DESIGN

What's a good design?

These are four questions we can ask before we design something:

- What is its purpose?
- Who will use it?
- Where will we use it?
- What will it look like?

Let's look at a chest of drawers as an example.

- A good chest of drawers should be big and strong enough for the clothes inside.
- It should not be too big or too small for the person using it.
- It should fit the space in the room.
- It should look nice.

Which chest of drawers has the best design? Why?

1

2

I can read and understand about the design process.

CYCLE

There are five stages to designing an item:

1 Identify the purpose

Identify the **purpose** of the design and any problems. For example, how can I make a table where I can eat dinner in the yard?

2 Research and imagine

Do some research. For example, what are the best **materials**? Does it need to be strong? What size, shape, or color should it be? What will it look like?

Draw simple designs on paper to record your research and ideas.

3 Design

Choose your best design and make models. You can use card, wood, or a 3D printer to make your model. Or you can use a computer to make a 3D model on screen. Then make a **prototype** to test the design.

4 Test the design

Test your prototype. Identify any problems and think of solutions. Discuss these with other people. How can you **improve** it?

5 Redesign

Think about your test and improve your design!

Good designs can be fun and beautiful.

1 7.9 **Listen. Why did Flo design a new bag?**

2 7.10 **Listen again and choose.**

1 How did she design her new bag?
   a She made a model. b She drew a picture.
2 What material did she use for her first design?
   a soft wool b old T-shirts
3 What material did she choose for her redesign?
   a the old plastic bag b some leather

Listening strategy

After listening, reread your answers to check that they make sense. Then listen again to check any answers you're not sure about.

MINI-PROJECT

3 Design an everyday item.

THINK What kind of item do you want to design? Think of some ideas with a friend.

PLAN Choose an idea, and discuss the four design questions.
Workbook page 84

SHARE Present your redesigned item to the class.

I can design an everyday item.

LESSON 9
Writing project

A comic strip

1 Read and write.

1 Where would you see this type of text? ______________________
2 Is the story real or imaginary? ______________________
3 Is the story told through words, pictures, or both? ______________________

2 Read again. Where is this information? Match.

1 Oliver and Amy are sorry.
2 It's Amy's red sock.
3 Mom and Dad are gardening.

a In a picture
b In a speech bubble.
c In a caption.

Writing focus

In comic strips and graphic stories, we use a sequence of pictures with speech bubbles and captions to tell the story.

Let's write!

3 Write a comic strip.

Think Think of an idea for a short comic strip story.

- Where and when is it set?
- Who are the characters?
- What is the main event?

My story is set in modern times.

Tip

Self-management: drafting and storyboarding

First, write and draw your comic strip in pencil. Add notes for the dialogue. Then check your work and make any changes. Once you are happy, go over your work in pen.

Get ready Plan your story. Answer these questions.

What is happening?

What will you show in the pictures?

What are the characters saying?

1 Noor is cleaning the floor when the doorbell rings.

2 Noor opens the door. It's Sayid. He's carrying the groceries.

3 Sayid falls on the wet floor. He drops the groceries.

4 Groceries fall on Noor's head. It looks funny.

Plan and write Plan your storyboard and write your comic strip. **Workbook** page 85

I can write a comic strip.

You can do it!

1 Complete the questions. Then listen and complete the answers. 7.11

1 Q: What ___was___ she doing when the phone rang?
A: She was ___sweeping___ the floor when the phone rang.

2 Q: What ____________ you doing when the door opened?
A: I was ____________ upstairs when the door opened.

3 Q: What were they doing ____________ the vase broke?
A: They were ____________ the cottage when the vase broke.

4 Q: What was he ____________ when the teacher arrived?
A: He was ____________ math when the teacher arrived.

2 Read and match.

1	Maurice picked a flower	a	to buy groceries.
2	I went to the hallway	b	to rescue the boy.
3	She went to the market	c	to give to Belle.
4	The firefighter broke the window	d	to get my school bag.

(1 – c)

Let's talk! What lessons do you learn in everyday life?

3 Tell a friend how accepting you're wrong can make a difference.

at home · at school · with friends · with family · with teammates

Movie quiz

1. What does the old woman do to the prince?
2. What says hello to Maurice at the castle?

I can ...

- use words related to household objects and chores ☐
- talk about why I did something ☐
- accept when I am wrong and say sorry ☐
- write a comic strip ☐

I completed Unit 7!

Go online
Big Project

8 Enjoy the music!

What kinds of music make you happy?

Look, think, and wonder.

1. What can you see?
2. Can you play any of these instruments?
3. How do you feel about music?

Vocabulary

1 saxophone
2 double bass
3 keyboard
4 electric guitar
5 trombone
6 violin

1 (8.1) **Match the words to the pictures. Then listen, check, and repeat.**

→ Which instruments are played with your mouth?

I can use words for musical instruments.

SOUL Storyboard

2 Watch the video and answer.

Finding happiness

1. Which instrument does Dorothea play?
2. *"Lost in the music."* What makes Joe feel like this?
3. Which other small things make Joe feel happy?

Self-awareness

3 Listen and write.

Joe is a music teacher. In the school band, some students play the guitar, the drums, and the trumpet. Connie is good at playing the **1** trombone, but she doesn't play the **2** ______________ . Joe goes to a jazz club. The band is awesome. Dorothea Williams plays the **3** ______________ . Another woman in the band plays the **4** ______________ . It's a string instrument. A **5** ______________ is a string instrument, too. Joe's favorite musical instrument is the piano. Do you think he plays the **6** ______________ , too?

4 Which musical instrument do you like best? Why?

I like the trombone best because it's loud and fun.

LESSON 2
Vocabulary

1 What musical instruments do you know?

2 Read and listen. Then match. 8.3

School Band Auditions

I love listening to music and playing the keyboard. I want to play in the school band!

Do you want to play in the school band?

We play a lot of different types of music, from modern 1 **pop** music to 2 **classical** music.

Do you play the trombone, trumpet, or saxophone? You will love 3 **jazz**!

Do you like to dance and play an instrument at the same time? Try 4 **Latin**!

We often use the computer lab to make 5 **rap** and 6 **electronic** music.

You can use our drum room to play loud 7 **rock** music.

Let's play some 8 **reggae** and imagine we're on the beach!

Come to the Music Room at 12 p.m. on Friday! **Don't forget your musical instrument.**

3 Write for you.

I like Latin music. It makes me feel excited.

I like ______________ . It makes me feel ______________ .

I don't like ______________ . It makes me feel ______________ .

4 Mime and guess.

Are you playing the electric guitar?

Yes, I am.

Is it rock music?

Talk buddies

Say what you know before you guess:

I know (you are playing the guitar).

I think (it looks upbeat).

Is it (jazz)?

I can use words for types of music.

Disney · PIXAR SOUL

1 8B Watch, read, and circle.

1. Joe and 22 go to Joe's **school** / **apartment**.
2. There's a **double bass** / **saxophone** in the living room.
3. Connie plays the **trumpet** / **trombone**.
4. Connie doesn't want to play **jazz** / **classical music** anymore.
5. 22 sits on the sidewalk in front of the **Latin** / **jazz** club.

2 8B Watch again. Read and write *T* (True) or *F* (False).

1. Cats would rather sleep in cold places than warm places. F
2. Joe would rather play the double bass than the piano. ____
3. 22 would rather spend time with Connie than with Joe. ____
4. The little girl would rather hop than walk. ____
5. The women in the café would rather eat than laugh. ____

3 Read, think, and say with a friend.

Grammar Heroes page 126

Preferences				
I / You / He / She / They / We	would rather	listen to jazz	than	pop.
		eat pizza		burgers.
		play the piano		the violin.
		hop		walk.
		laugh		eat.

4 Say and guess with a friend.

Ash
☺ electric guitar
😐 keyboard
☹ double bass

Emily
☺ electronic music
😐 pop music
☹ classical music

Flo
☺ doing judo
😐 dancing
☹ playing the piano

Pablo
☺ playing rap music
😐 playing reggae
☹ playing Latin music

She would rather listen to pop music than classical music.

It's Emily!

5 Write your preferences. Tell a friend.

I would rather listen to pop music than rock music.

I would rather play the electric guitar than the keyboard.

I can talk about preferences.

1 Look at the story and answer.

1 What do you think the story is about?
2 What kind of concert are they going to?
3 Do you like to write about the things you do?

2 Listen and read. Who's the author?

Do you like going to **concerts**? Well, I do!
One morning at breakfast, I read that my favorite rock band was coming to town.
Mom asked, "How much does a ticket cost?"
"$40," I said.
"How long is the concert?" asked Dad.
"Two hours. It's in the park near the beach.
You have to hear the **drummer** – she's awesome!
Can we go, please?"
Dad said, "Hmmm. It's a little expensive. I would rather listen to jazz than rock music, but I know you love this band so … let's go!"

I was excited about the concert. When we arrived at the park, there were too many people. We had to stand far away, and I couldn't see the band. I sat on my dad's shoulders. "Can you see the band, Victoria? How many **dancers** are there?" asked Dad.
"I don't know! I can't see the **singer**, the musicians, or the dancers," I said.

"That's OK. Don't feel sad. We can still dance and have fun," said Dad.
I felt shy. I didn't want to dance.
The people around us were talking and laughing loudly. I couldn't hear the music.
I felt sad. I couldn't see or hear my favorite band. I said, "It's too noisy. I don't like it here. Can we please go?"
My mom gave me a hug and said, "It's OK. It's a beautiful evening. Let's go to the beach."

We walked along the sand. The ocean was calm and quiet. There were hundreds of stars in the dark sky. I felt happy now.
We sat down and ate some pizza. It was delicious.

"Listen!" said Mom. We could hear a drummer. It sounded amazing.
Then we heard a guitar, a trombone, and a saxophone. A group of friends were playing Latin music and dancing.
"Let's dance!" said Dad. We started dancing.
I wasn't shy here on this beautiful beach. I laughed and said to my parents, "I would rather be at the beach than the concert. Small things are the best! I feel much happier."
"And how much does it cost?" said Dad.
"Nothing!"

Think!

Which musical instruments do the musicians in the rock band play? Look and check your answers on page 126.

3 Read again and write.

1 Why is Victoria excited in the morning?
Her favorite rock band is coming to town.

2 Would Victoria's dad rather listen to jazz or rock music?
____

3 Why doesn't Victoria dance at the concert?
____

4 What do they do on the beach?
____

4 Vocabulary Complete the definitions. Then match.

1 concert : a music show
2 ______________ : a person dancing
3 ______________ : a person playing the drums
4 ______________ : a person singing

a  1

b  ___

c  ___

d  ___

5 Discuss with a friend.

Finding happiness

1. What big thing does Victoria think will make her happy?
2. Name three small things Victoria enjoys at the beach.
3. Why would Victoria rather dance on the beach than at the concert?

Self-awareness

I can read a personal narrative about finding happiness.

1 Listen and read. What kind of music does the band play?

8.5

Look, Ash.
An Electric Sound concert!

Oh … is that your favorite band?

Yes, it is. I would rather listen to electronic music than pop.

How many musicians and singers are there?

There are three musicians. Gino plays the keyboard, Yasmin plays the electric guitar, and there's a drummer, too – Josh. The singer is Rita. She's an awesome dancer, too.

How long is the concert?

It's 90 minutes long.

How much does it cost?

It costs $10 for a ticket. Do you want to come?

OK! It sounds fun.

2 Read again and write.

1 How many musicians are there?

____

2 How long is the concert?

____

3 How much does a ticket cost?

____

3 Read, think, and say with a friend. Find similar sentences in the dialog.

Grammar Heroes page 126

***How* questions**		
How	long	is the concert? is the movie?
	many	singers are there?
	much	does a ticket cost? does the cake cost?

Speak up!

4 Listen and repeat. Underline the stressed words.

8.6

1 How long is the music lesson?
2 How many violins are there?
3 How can we get to the concert?
4 How much does the trombone cost?

5 Complete the music survey. Then ask and answer.

Music Survey

1 *How often do you go to a concert?*
2 *How many musicians and singers are in your favorite band?*
3 *What is your favorite song?*
4 *How long is your favorite song?*

How often do you go to a concert?

I go to a concert once a year.

I can ask questions with *How* + adjective.

Extra Lesson

Go online Phonics

Finding happiness

1 What small things help characters in the unit find happiness?

2 Listen and read. Then answer.

8.7

1 Where are the chemicals made?
2 How do they make you feel?

Reflect Can you think of a small thing that makes you feel happy right now?

Happy Chemicals

Can you think of something that made you smile or laugh this week? Why do small things, like walking in the sunlight, make us feel happy? When you do small, fun activities, your brain makes happy chemicals:

1 **Dopamine:**
- finishing your homework
- learning to play an instrument

2 **Oxytocin:**
- hugging your family
- playing with pets

3 **Serotonin:**
- doing a little exercise
- spending time in sunlight

4 **Endorphins:**
- laughing
- doing a lot of exercise

Your brain makes these happy chemicals when you find happiness in small things.

3 Write for you. Which chemical will your brain release? Write the number.

What can you do to feel happy when ...

a you are bored inside because it's raining? ➜ ____________________ ☐
b a concert you were excited about is cancelled? ➜ ____________________ ☐
c you are stressed at school? ➜ ____________________ ☐

4 Reflect on one small thing that makes you happy. Discuss with a friend.

When I feel bored, I play the violin. It makes me feel awesome!

That's great. I feel happier when I ride my bike.

Useful Language
Something small that makes me happy is when …
I feel great/awesome when ….

Self-awareness I can understand what makes me feel happy.

LESSON 7
My world

Science

Physics and music

1 Read, listen, and answer.

8.8

1 Name three things sound can travel through.
2 What parts of the body do we use to hear sounds?
3 Which has a higher pitch – thunder or a mouse?

Reading strategy
Diagrams and illustrations help you identify and understand difficult vocabulary and the main ideas of a non-fiction text.

2 Vocabulary Read and complete.

The strings on a violin **1** vibrate the air around it. These **2** ______ travel through the air to our ears. They are called **3** ______ . They vibrate the **4** ______ and send a message to the brain. We can hear the sound. The **5** ______ can be loud or quiet, and the **6** ______ can be high or low.

3 Order the musical instruments into wind, string, and percussion.

flute violin trumpet trombone
double bass saxophone drums

Disney **In the real world**

Many characters in *Soul* play musical instruments, but how do we hear the sounds they play?

Sound is all around us

We hear birds singing, musicians playing, people laughing, and cars moving.

What is sound?

Sound travels as waves of **vibrations** called **sound waves**. These vibrations can travel:

- **through the air**
- **through liquids (like water)**
- **through solids (like wood, glass, and metal)**

Sound travels faster through water than through air.

Sound vibrations travel into your ear and then to your **eardrum**. Your eardrum **vibrates** and sends messages up to your brain. You hear the vibrations as sound.

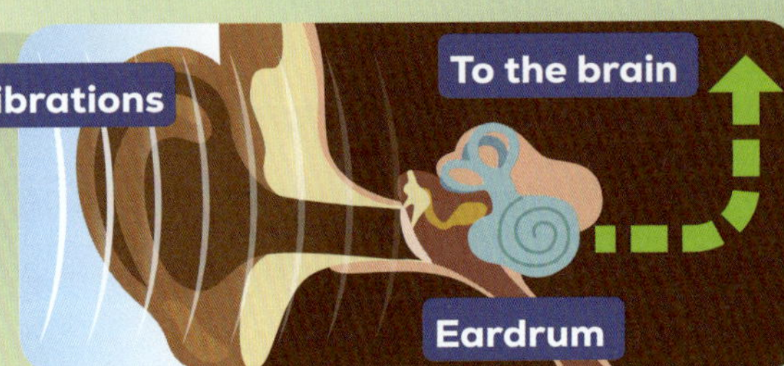

What is volume?

The **volume** of sound is how loud or quiet it is.
Big sound waves are louder than small sound waves.
Hit a drum hard to make big vibrations. These make loud sounds.
Hit the drum softly to make small vibrations. These make quiet sounds.

I can read and understand about sound.

How do musical instruments make sound?

When musicians play instruments, they make vibrations. Different instruments make sound vibrations in different ways:

- **The air going into wind instruments (like trombones).**
- **Moving the strings on string instruments (like violins, guitars, and double basses).**
- **Hitting percussion instruments (like drums).**

You can feel the vibrations when you play musical instruments!

What is pitch?

The pitch of a sound is how high or low it is. A high sound has a high pitch. A low sound has a low pitch.

Short vibrations make high pitch sounds. Long vibrations make low pitch sounds.

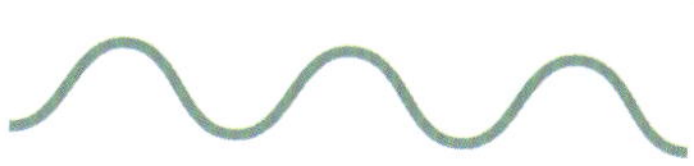

This sound wave shows a low pitch.

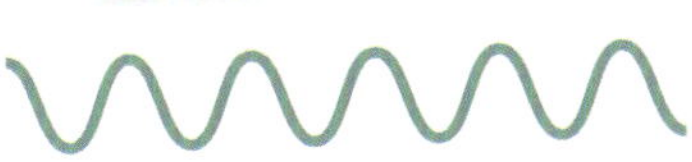

This sound wave shows a high pitch.

1 8.9 **Listen and circle three things Emily and Ash hear.**

cars   a violin   a trombone

classical music   rap music

Listening strategy

Background noises tell you where a conversation is happening. This will help you predict what the conversation is about.

2 8.10 **Listen again and check (✓).**

Listening walk

Sound	Rock music	Trucks	Birds	Violin
Loud				
Quiet				

MINI-PROJECT

3 **Research a musical instrument.**

THINK Choose an instrument you don't know anything about.

PLAN Research your musical instrument.
Workbook page 96

SHARE Present your poster to the class.

Liuqin
This is a string instrument from China.

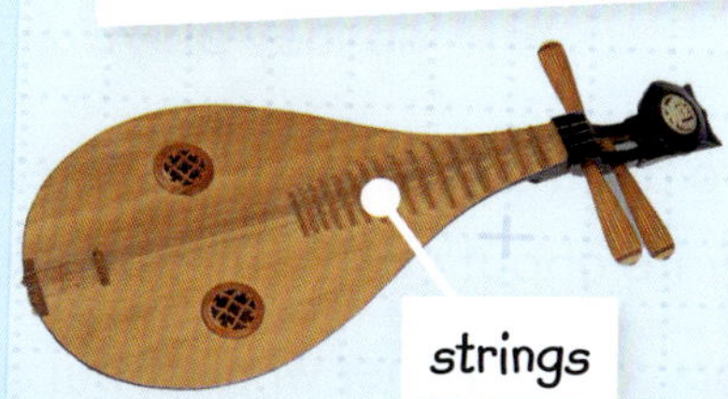

The strings vibrate the air.
It has a high pitch. It can be loud or quiet.
You usually play classical music on it.

I can research a musical instrument.

A review

1 Read and circle.

1 Where would you read this text type? **textbook / comic book / online**
2 How long are the concerts? **2 hours / 1 hour / 3 hours**
3 How much does a ticket cost? **$5 / $4 / $6**

Band Review

Super K

by Emily Smith POP MUSIC

Super K is a famous pop band. There are four musicians in the band. Joey is a singer and plays the guitar. Lisa plays the electric guitar. Kim is the drummer. Fei plays the keyboard. There are three dancers at most of their concerts. They play concerts every Saturday. The concerts are about one hour long, and a ticket costs $5.

I would usually rather listen to electronic music than pop, but I like Super K. I feel happy when I listen to their music. I like dancing to their songs because the music is fast. My favorite Super K song is *Jump up!*

I give Super K ★★★★☆. Go see them soon!

2 Read again. Find and write.

Band name: Super K
Type of music: ____________
Author's opinion ____________
Rating: ____________ stars

Writing focus

In a review, we give our opinion. Make sure you give a reason for your opinion:
*I like it **because** it's fast.*
*I don't like it **because** it's too loud.*

Let's write!

3 Write a review for a class music blog.

Think Choose bands or music that you have listened to recently. What do you know about them?

What's the band's best song?

What musical instruments do they play?

Get ready Work in a group to discuss your music preferences. Decide who will write about each music genre.

I'd rather listen to rap than pop.

I'd rather write about a reggae group.

Plan and write Write your review for the class music blog.

Workbook page 97

Tip

Collaboration: negotiating topics

A good class music blog will cover different opinions and types of music! Talk to your group to make sure you don't all write about the same things.

Summer Vibes
Best song: Sunrise to Sunset
Reggae music
Singer: Cherry Guitar: Junior
Drummer: Devon
Rating: ★★★

I can write a review.

YOU CAN DO IT!

1 Listen and write. 8.11

1 Joe would rather play the ___piano___ than teach band practice.
2 We would rather play reggae than ______________ music.
3 I would rather play the ______________ than the saxophone.
4 They would rather play ______________ than pop.
5 She would rather go to a music ______________ than the movie theatre.

2 Read and write. Then match.

1 How ___much___ does a ticket cost?
2 How ______________ is the concert?
3 How ______________ singers are there?
4 ______________ many dancers are there?
5 How ______________ does a violin cost?

a It's 90 minutes long.
b It costs $20.
c There are five dancers.
d It costs $400.
e There are two singers.

Let's talk! What kinds of music make you happy?

3 Tell a friend how small things bring happiness.

hanging out with a friend
listening to music
eating ice cream
riding my bike
reading a good book

Movie quiz

1 What does Joe teach?
2 Which musical instrument does Connie play?

I can ...

- use words related to music ☐
- talk about my preferences ☐
- understand what makes me feel happy ☐
- write a review ☐

I completed Unit 8!

Go online
Big Project

9 Adventure is out there!

Where can we find adventure?

Look, think, and wonder.

1. What can you see?
2. Where do you think Russell and Carl are?
3. What do you think Russell has in his backpack?

1 (9.1) **Match the words to the pictures. Then listen, check, and repeat.**

→ Do you have any of these things?

Vocabulary

1 rope
2 uniform
3 flashlight
4 map
5 compass
6 binoculars

I can use words about outdoor items.

Storyboard

2 Watch the video and answer.

What's stopping you?

1. *"Adventure is out there!"* What adventures does Ellie dream of?
2. Is Carl young or old when he travels to South America?
3. How does Russell feel about going on an adventure?

Self-management

3 Listen and write.

Carl uses a **1** ___map___ and a **2** ______________ to fly his house to South America. Russell wears a **3** ______________ and has **4** ______________ around his neck. Russell has a **5** ______________ in his backpack. Maybe he has a **6** ______________ in it, too? Together, they're ready for an adventure!

4 You're going on an adventure. What are you going to take?

I'm going to take a flashlight and some chocolate.

LESSON 2
Vocabulary

1 What outdoor activities do you know?

use	climb	make	go	read	wear
a compass	a rope	a campfire	stargazing	a map	hiking boots

2 Read and listen. Then match.

Dear Mom and Dad,

Summer camp is amazing! I'm excited about the activities we're going to do.

Today, we **1** **put up a tent**. We're going to **2** **sleep in sleeping bags** tonight! Tomorrow, we're going to **3** **go canoeing** on the river. In the afternoon, we're going to make vegetable soup on the campfire. Then we're going to **4** **cook marshmallows**.

On Wednesday, we're going to **5** **go hiking** in the countryside. We're going to use a map to **6** **find the way**. We're going to climb a rope. Then I'm going to learn how to **7** **tie a knot**.

Let's **8** **stay at a campsite** together soon!

Love,

Pablo

I'm at summer camp with my friends. This is my postcard for Mom and Dad.

a) a food activity ___
b) a river activity ___
c) an activity you can do with rope ___
d) a walking activity ___
e) an activity you can do with a map ___
f) three things you do when camping 1 ___ ___

3 Write for you.

I want to stay at a campsite.

I want to ______________________.

I don't want to ______________________.

4 Describe and guess.

You can do this on a river.

Go canoeing!

Talk buddies

Don't know the answer? Ask for more information:

What does that mean?

Can you give me another example?

Can you tell me more?

I can use words for camping activities.

Disney · PIXAR UP

1 Watch, read, and circle. 9B

Carl and Russell arrived at Paradise Falls. Russell tried to climb the 1 **rope** / **tree** by himself. It was hard. At night, it rained and Russell's 2 **compass** / **uniform** was wet. They couldn't stay at a 3 **hotel** / **campsite**. They didn't have 4 **sleeping bags** / **a tent**. The next day was better – they found some cute birds.

2 Watch again. Read and write *T* (True) or *F* (False). 9B

1. Carl tried to climb the rope by himself. F
2. Russell and Carl made a campfire by themselves. ____
3. Russell put up the tent by himself. ____
4. Russell went canoeing by himself. ____

3 Read, think, and say with a friend.

Grammar Heroes page 127

by + reflexive pronouns			
I	made the uniform put up the tent read the map went hiking	by	myself.
He			himself.
She			herself.
We			ourselves.
They			themselves.

4 Say and guess with a friend.

1

2

3

4

She tied a knot by herself.

Picture 3!

5 Write what you did by yourself last weekend. Tell a friend.

I went to the park by myself.
We made dinner by ourselves.

I can talk about things I do by myself.

Barbara Hillary: Explorer 1931 – 2019

1 Look at the story and answer.

1 Is this historical fiction or a biography? How do you know?
2 What do you think the main character is like?
3 Do you know any famous explorers?

2 Listen and read. Why is Barbara Hillary famous?

When she was a little girl, Barbara Hillary lived in New York. Her mom was a cleaner and she worked long hours. They didn't have much money, but her mom bought Barbara a lot of books.

Barbara's favorite books were about **explorers**.

Barbara studied at university. Then she worked with older people in New York.

When she was 67, she stopped working. She wanted to travel by herself. Her first adventure was in Canada. She took photos of polar bears and went sledding.

After that, she read a lot of books about the **North Pole** and the **South Pole**. Barbara decided it was time for another adventure – to the North Pole!

First, she had to prepare.

She did a lot of exercise and learned to **ski**. That wasn't easy in New York. She hiked on the beach and pulled bags of sand by herself to become stronger.

Think!

What was Barbara's favorite book when she was a child? Look and check your answer on page 127.

Some people said to her, "You're too old," and "The polar bears could eat you," but Barbara didn't listen to them.

In 2007, she left New York and she traveled to Europe by herself. Then she traveled hundreds of kilometers north by helicopter. She put up a tent on the ice.

For about two weeks, she hiked and skied to the North Pole with a heavy backpack full of things like ... a sleeping bag  a flashlight  a compass  and maps. 

← Key items

Finally, she was at the top of the world. She was the first African-American woman to travel to the North Pole and she was 75 years old! Barbara loved the adventure. She was so happy and excited.

Four years later, Barbara wanted to be the first African-American woman to travel to the South Pole.

She overcame many challenges by herself to become the first woman to visit both Poles. It was difficult, but she didn't let anything stop her!

What adventures might you go on?

3 Read again and write.

1 What did Barbara Hillary want to do when she was 67?
She wanted to travel by herself.

2 Where did Barbara prepare for her adventure to the North Pole?
____

3 How old was Barbara when she traveled to the North Pole?
____

4 Where did Barbara go after the North Pole?
____

4 Vocabulary Look and write.

Barbara Hillary was an **1** explorer.

She taught herself to **2** __________.

Barbara is at the **3** __________.

The penguins are at the **4** __________.

5 Discuss with a friend.

What's stopping you?

1. How did Barbara Hillary become an explorer?
2. Why did some people think she shouldn't go to the North Pole?
3. Did she listen to them?

Self-management

I can read a biography about overcoming problems.

1 Listen and read. Where does Pablo want to go?

Hi, Pablo. Can you help me? Who was the first explorer to travel to the North and South Poles?

Hi, Emily. It was Roald Amundsen.

He looks serious! What adventures do you want to go on? Do you want to ski to the North Pole?

No. I don't like cold weather! I may go canoeing and hiking in the Amazon rainforest.

Great idea! You might see monkeys!

What about you? Do you want to be an explorer, too?

Yes, I do. I might explore the Sahara Desert. I could use a compass to find the way.

Wow! Just imagine – my friend the famous explorer!

You could come with me!

2 Read again and write.

1 Pablo may go canoeing and hiking.
2 Pablo might see ______ in the rainforest.
3 Emily could use a ______ to find the way.
4 Pablo could explore ______ with Emily.

3 Read, think, and say with a friend. Find similar sentences in the dialog.

Grammar Heroes page 127

may / might / could for possibility		
I / You / He / She We / They	may might could	go canoeing. explore the Sahara Desert. tie a knot. stay at a campsite

Speak up!

4 Listen and repeat. Draw arrows when the intonation goes up ↗ and down ↘ on the words in bold.

1 I **may** cook **marshmallows**.
2 They **won't** use **binoculars**.
3 We **might** put up the tent **now**.
4 He **can't** tie a knot by **himself**.

5 Circle the activities you might do. Then talk with a friend. Which ones might you both do?

go canoeing | stay at a campsite | cook marshmallows | use binoculars | read a map | catch fish

I might go canoeing.

Hmm, me too / not me!

I can talk about possible future activities.

Extra Lesson

Go online Phonics

What's stopping you?

1 How do characters in the unit overcome problems to achieve their goals?

2 Listen and read. Complete the bucket lists. 9.7

Overcoming problems

Step 1: Understand the problem
Think of something that you'd like to do. What's stopping you from doing it?

Step 2: Make a plan
Think of solutions to these problems. Break the problem down into small tasks.

Think of these small tasks as steps on a ladder. This is your goal ladder.

Step 3: Put the plan into action
Don't let anything stop you!

Step 4: Review
Can you learn from your experience?

Emily's Vacation Bucket List

I want to ...

a) go stargazing in the countryside
b) ______________ on a river
c) go rock climbing

Pablo's Vacation Bucket List

I want to ...

a) ______________ to a volcano
b) do archery
c) swim in the ocean

Useful Language
I might fail.
I may not enjoy it.
I might hurt myself.
It could be ...

3 Match the problems to things on the bucket lists in 2.

1. The water might be too cold. Pablo, c
2. It might be dangerous. My arms aren't strong enough. ______________
3. I'm scared of the dark. I don't like being outdoors at night. ______________
4. I might fall into the river. ______________
5. I may not enjoy it. I could fall since I'm not good at climbing. ______________
6. I might fail. I might get lost. ______________

4 Make your adventure camp bucket list. Use the steps in 2. Discuss with a friend.

I want to go hiking by myself, but I might get lost. I'm going to take a compass and my cell phone.

Good plan!

Reflect
Have you overcome a problem to do something exciting?

Self-management I can set goals and overcome problems.

Maps and measurements

1 Read, listen, and answer. (9.8)

1 Write the missing word:
north south east ______

2 Choose the things you might need to measure distance on a map.
a ruler b flashlight c scale
d rope e string

3 How many meters are there in a kilometer?

Reading strategy
When learning to read a map, first look at the key or legend which explains the symbols.

2 Vocabulary Read and complete.

1 We can use a ruler to ___measure___ a short distance.

2 We usually measure a long ____________ in kilometers.

3 A ____________ helps us measure distances on maps.

4 There are 100,000 ____________ in a kilometer.

5 In the morning, the sun rises in the ____________ .

6 In the evening, the sun sets in the ____________ .

3 Look at the scale. How far is three centimeters on the map in real life?

Disney **In the real world**

In *Up*, Carl and Russell travel a long distance to Paradise Falls. They use maps, a compass, and GPS to find their way.

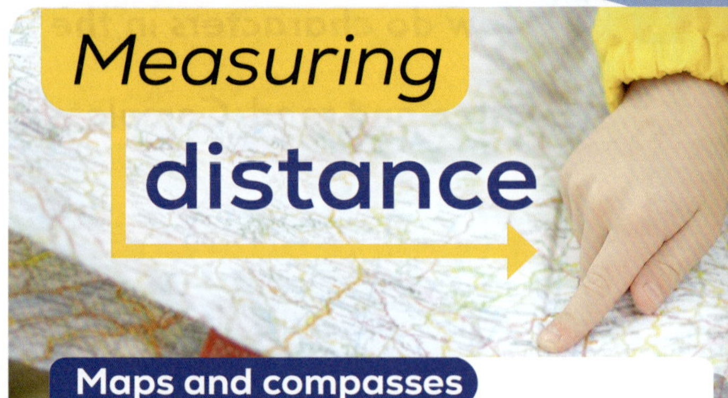

Measuring distance

Maps and compasses

Maps give us information about what a place looks like. They also tell us the **distance** between places.

A compass tells us where to find north, south, **east**, and **west**. On a map, north is always at the top. You can use a map and a compass together to find your way.

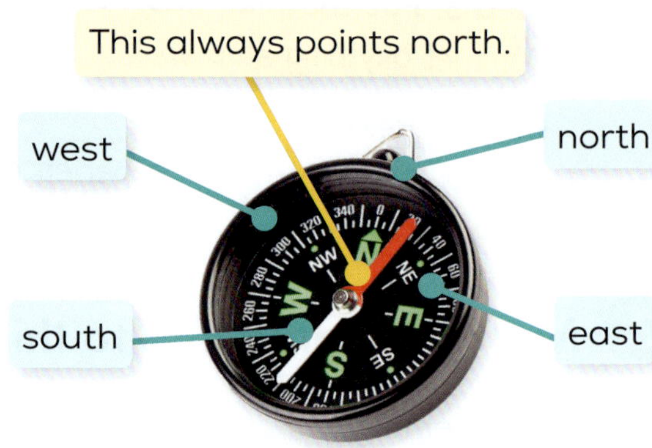

Measuring distance on maps

A **scale** helps you find out the real distance between places on a map.

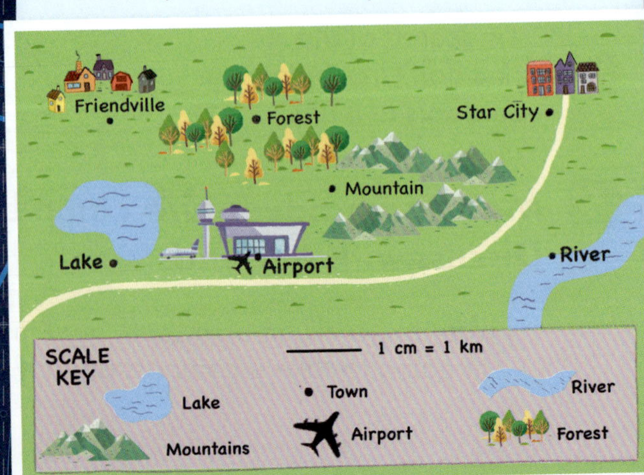

I can read and understand about measuring distances on maps.

Step 1: Find the scale on the map. This is usually in **centimeters**.

Step 2: Find the place you want to travel to on your map. **Measure** the distance between where you are and the place you want to be on the map. Use a ruler to measure this in centimeters.

Step 3: Use the scale to find out how many kilometers this is in real life. For example, on this scale, one centimeter is one kilometer.

Remember!
1 kilometer = 100,000 centimeters, or 1,000 meters

How can we work out distances when we can't travel in a straight line? For example, a road between an airport and a city might go around a mountain or a lake.

Step 1: Use string to follow the road on the map. Mark the start and the end (e.g. the city).

Step 2: Measure the string in centimeters. Repeat step 3 above!

GPS

Today, we often use GPS on our cell phones to find our way. These are like electronic maps. They have a compass, too, and a scale to measure distance. They can tell you how many kilometers away a place is and how long it will take to arrive there. You can make the map bigger or smaller. You can even see real photos of places all over the world.

1 9.9 **Listen and check (✓). What did Pablo do by himself on his last vacation?**

read a map	◯	put up a tent	◯
use a compass	◯	tie a knot	◯

2 9.10 **Listen again and complete. Then draw the route.**

bridge ~~east~~ field north path river west

Listening strategy
When you are listening for missing words, underline the key words in the text first. Then listen for those words.

Geocaching directions

Hike **1** *east* across the **2** ______________ .
Walk **3** ______________ up the **4** ______________ .
Hike **5** ______________ along the **6** ______________ .
The box is on the **7** ______________ .

8 1______________ = 1 kilometer

MINI-PROJECT

3 **Create a map-reading adventure.**

THINK What will you hide and where will you hide it? Discuss in your group.

PLAN Draw a map with a scale and an arrow pointing north.
Workbook page 108

SHARE Exchange your maps with another group. Do the map-reading adventure.

I can create a map-reading challenge.

An adventure book

1 Read and write.

1 Who's the author of the adventure book?

____

2 Where will she go?

____

3 What might she take with her?

____

2 Look at the text and find:

Which verbs does Emily use for:

1 headings in her text?

____

2 things she isn't sure about?

__________ __________

3 things she definitely wants to do?

____

Writing focus

Use *may*, *might*, or *could* for possible plans in the future. We use *going to* for more definite plans or ambitions.

MY ADVENTURE BOOK
by Emily

Where will I go?

I'll travel to Central America. I may visit a volcano. I might stay at a campsite near a waterfall.

Who will I go with?

I'll go with my best friend. I might also take my dog.

How will I do it?

Skills

I'm going to tie difficult knots by myself. I'm also going to use a compass and a map. We might need to go hiking by ourselves.

Adventures

I'm going to use binoculars to find exciting animals. Maybe I could go canoeing on the Amazon River!

Let's write!

Tip

Presentation: identifying and explaining key points

Summarize your adventure. Identify and explain the main points. Show your photos and explain why they're special to you.

3 Write an adventure book.

Think What adventures might you have?

I may go to India! I might go hiking in the Himalayas.

Get ready Work with a partner to answer these questions:

Where will you go?
- Canada
- China
- South America

Who will you go with?
- My friend
- My parents
- My brother

What skills will you need?
- reading a map
- using binoculars
- mountain biking

Plan and write Write your adventure book and present it to the class! Workbook page 109

Present Present your adventure book to the class.

I can write and present an adventure book.

You can do it!

1 Listen, write, and circle. (9.11)

1 We __could__ go on **a rollercoaster** / **an adventure**.

2 I ________ cook **potatoes** / **marshmallows** on a campfire.

3 We ________ sleep in **a bed** / **a sleeping bag**.

4 I ________ hike **north** / **south** to the river.

5 We ________ use a **compass** / **map** when exploring.

Test your progress with English Benchmark Young Learners

2 Read and write.

~~tie~~ put up use go ski

1 I __tied__ the knot by __myself__ .

2 You ________ the tent by ________ .

3 He ________ the compass by ________ .

4 We ________ canoeing by ________ .

5 She ________ by ________ .

Let's talk!

Where can we find adventure?

3 Tell a friend about one adventure you really want to have.

around the neighborhood

in the city

while camping

outdoors

Movie quiz

1 Where did Carl and Ellie want to go?

2 How do Carl and Russell travel?

I can ...

- use words related to the outdoors ☐
- talk about things I do by myself ☐
- set goals and overcome problems ☐
- write an adventure book ☐

I completed Unit 9!

Go online
Big Project

Grammar

1 Read and complete. Then read and circle.

~~did~~ is can't ago

Simple Past with *ago*

What did	you / he / she	**do**	an hour a week	**ago**?
I / He / She	**lived** in a village **was** a warrior **worked** in a team		a week a few years two months	______ .

1 We use the Simple Past + *ago* to talk about things that happened in the **past** / **present**.

2 We put *ago* at the **beginning** / **end** of the questions and answers.

Tag questions

You **know** the Mulan story,	**don't you**?	We **don't** have to bring food,	**do we**?
We **can** meet at the museum,	______ **we**?	We **can't** take photos in the museum,	**can we**?
Mulan **is** Hua Zhou's daughter,	**isn't she**?	He **isn't** the oldest son,	______ **he**?

3 We add question tags like *do we?* to a statement to make it into **an answer** / **a question**.

4 The main verb and the verb in the question tag are **sometimes** / **never** the same.

Present	Past
be	was/were
do	did
eat	ate
feel	felt
find	found
have	had
go	went
ride	rode
see	saw
sleep	slept
take	took
write	wrote

2 Think of three things you did two days ago and write.

I played soccer two days ago.
I went to my friend's house two days ago.
I ...

3 How well do you know your partner? Ask and answer using tag questions.

pets | brothers and sisters | hobbies | likes | abilities

You get 100 points for each one you get right.

How many points can you can and your partner get in 5 minutes?

☐ correct statements

☐ points

You have a pet cat, don't you?

Grammar

1 **Read and complete. Then read and circle.**

couldn't ~~was~~ could were

is / was + like

What	**was** he / she	**like** when	he / she was	five? younger?
	were you		you ______	
I / He / She	**was** / **wasn't**	friendly. hard-working.		
You	**were** / **weren't**			
What	**are** you **is** he / she	**like now**?		
I'm / He**'s** / She**'s**	confident.			

1 We use *is* + *like* to talk about someone's personality **now** / **in the past**.

2 We use *was* + *like* to talk about someone's personality **now** / **in the past**.

could / couldn't

______	he / she	snowboard tie your shoelaces	**when**	he / she	**was**	four? younger?
	you			you	**were**	
Yes,	I / he / she	**could**.	No,	I / he / she	______ .	
I / He / She	**could** **couldn't**	do a cartwheel play soccer	**when**	I / he / she	**was**	four. younger.
You				you	**were**	

3 We use *could* / *couldn't* to talk about the **present** / **past**.

4 We use *could* to talk about something we **were** / **weren't** able to do in the past. We use *couldn't* to talk about something we **were** / **weren't** able to do in the past.

2 **What were you like when you were seven? What could you do? Write two more things in the chart.**

	Me	My friend
patient		
shy		
hardworking		
tie my shoelaces		
whistle a tune		
do a cartwheel		

3 **Complete for you. Then ask and answer. Which answers are the same as your partner's?**

What were you like when you were seven?

I was friendly.

Me too!

Think!

He was away traveling in the USA.

Grammar

1 Read and complete. Then read and circle.

take shouldn't ~~have~~ feel

Talking about illness		
What's the matter?		
My	hand / ankle / wrist / knee	**hurts**.
I have a / an	stomach ache / headache / earache / toothache / backache cold / sore throat / cough.	
I **feel** I **don't** ________	dizzy / sick. good.	

should / shouldn't		
I You He / She We / They	**should** ________	**see** a doctor. **stay** in bed. ________ some medicine. **put on** a bandage. **go** to basketball practice.

1 We use ***hurts*** / ***feels*** when we are talking about a part of the body.

2 We use ***feel*** / ***have*** when we are talking about illnesses.

3 We use *should* to **give advice** / **talk about possibility**.

4 We use *should* / *shouldn't* + **infinitive** / **-*ing* form**.

2 Imagine you're sick. Write about your illness.

I have a headache.
I feel dizzy.
I ...

3 Look at A and B. Ask and answer to find out which illness you each have. Give advice using *should* / *shouldn't*.

I have a sore throat.

You should take some medicine.

Student A

have a headache	________
toothache	________
________	✓ put on a bandage
________	✗ go rock-climbing

Student B

________	✓ take some medicine
________	✗ eat candy
wrist hurts	________
feel dizzy	________

Think!

She sees the bag and feathers.

Grammar

1 Read and complete. Then read and circle.

be ~~will~~ There won't

will for future predictions		
Will	I / you / we /	**have** robotic teachers? **travel** by hovertrain?
Yes,	I / you / we /	will .
No,		**won't**.
I/ You / We	**will**	**ride** electric motorcycles.
	________	**use** AI speakers in school. **drive** electric cars.

1 We use *will* to ***predict future events*** / ***describe the past***.
2 We use ***will*** / ***won't*** with *Yes* answers.

will for future predictions			
What	**will**	schools teachers	________ **like**?
________	**will**	**be**	artificial food. wireless schools.
	won't		

3 We use *What will* to **ask** / **answer** questions about the future.
4 We end these *What will …?* questions with **infinitive +** ***like?*** / ***-ing*** **form +** ***like?***

2 Write three predictions for the future.

We will have robotic teachers. There won't be artificial food. I will ...

3 Ask and answer to find out your partner's future job.

Will you be ...	Will you work ...	Will you ...	Will you be a ...
caring	patient	sporty	brave
in a school	in a hospital	at a sports center	at a fire station
teach people	help people	exercise everyday	rescue people
teacher	doctor	athlete	firefighter

Think!

She will send tomato seeds.

Grammar

1 Read and complete. Then read and circle.

~~does~~ enough like many

Describing something

What <u>does</u> it	**look / sound / feel / smell / taste**	**like?**

It	**feels** **smells** **tastes** **looks** **sounds**	hard. horrible. delicious. __________ a heart. like a bird.

1 We use *look + like a* to talk about the **difference** / **similarity** between two things.

2 We use **an adjective** / **a noun** after *taste + like*.

Quantifiers

There's	**too much**	frosting. paper.
There isn't	__________	
There are	**too** __________	sails. colors.
There aren't	**enough**	

3 Quantifiers are words that tell us **how many there are** / **where things are**.

4 We use quantifiers **before** / **after** nouns.

2 Ask and answer. Describe a food or thing and ask your partner to guess what it is.

What does it look like?

It looks like an orange.

What does it smell like?

It smells like lemons.

Think!

The cakes looked like fruit - pineapples and watermelons.

3 Think about your classroom. Write your opinion using too *much* / *many* / *not enough*.

There's too many desks.

There aren't enough windows.

There's too much dust.

There isn't enough paper.

There ...

Grammar

1 Read and complete. Then read and circle.

worried ~~have~~ has about

have to / don't have to

I / You / We / They	have to	**wait** in line.
	don't have to	**buy** a ticket.
He / She	________ **to**	**stay** together.
	doesn't have to	**go** to the entrance.

Adjectives and prepositions

I'm / He's / She's	________ **about**	the bumper cars.
	scared of	the exam.
What	are you	**excited** ________ ?
	is he / she	**interested in**?

1 We use *have to* to talk about things we **need to** / **don't need to** do.

2 We use *have* / *has* to + **past participle** / **infinitive form.**

3 We use prepositions to link the **adjective** / **adverb** and the noun.

4 We put the preposition **before** / **after** the noun.

2 Ask and answer to find out which rules you and your friend have to follow.

You have to wait in line.

You don't have to sit down.

Student A

Student B

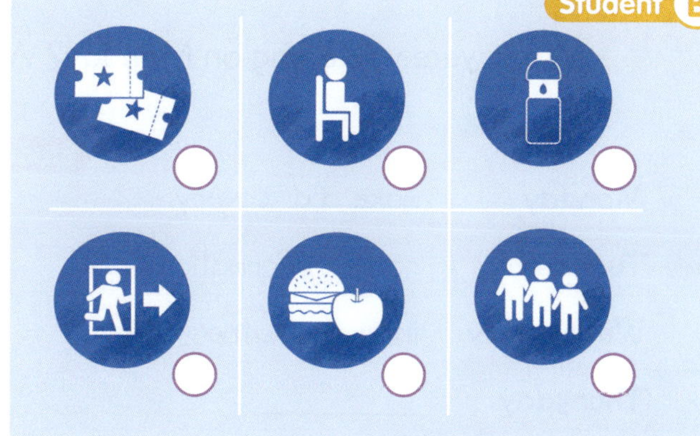

3 Write three sentences using *worried about*, *scared of* and *interested in*. Compare with a partner.

I'm scared of spiders.

I'm interested in science.

I'm worried about...

Think!

Mom is a doctor.

Grammar

1 Read and complete. Then read and circle.

was were ~~doing~~ weren't

Past Progressive

What	**were**	you / they	doing	at 9.30 a.m./ p.m.? on Monday? in the morning?
	was	he / she		
They	______	**solving** a mystery. **gathering** information. **looking** at a notebook.		
I / He / She	**was**			

Past Progressive – questions and short answers

Was	he / she	**doing** judo? **cracking** codes? **interviewing** teams? **following** clues?	Yes,	I / he / she	______ .
				they	**were**.
Were	you / they		No,	I / he / she	**wasn't**.
				they	______ .

1 We use the Past Progressive to describe things that were happening in the **past** / **present**.

2 We use *was* / *were* + **imperative** / **-*ing* form** to form the Past Progressive.

3 We use Past Progressive questions to ask about things that were happening in the **future** / **past**.

4 We use ***was*** / ***were*** after *he* in Past Progressive short answers.

2 Ask and answer to find out what you and your friend were doing each day.

What were you doing on Monday? Were you looking for clues?

No, I wasn't. I was …

Student A

Monday	make a discovery
Tuesday	gather information
Wednesday	interview witnesses
Thursday	______
Friday	______
Saturday	______

Student B

Monday	______
Tuesday	______
Wednesday	______
Thursday	crack the codes
Friday	solve a mystery
Saturday	watch the news

Think!

The thief also took a museum security badge.

Grammar

1 Read and complete. Then read and circle.

did to ~~were~~ when

Interrupted Past

What	**was**	I / he / she	**doing**	**when**	the people **arrived**? the phone **rang**?
	were	you / they /we			
I / He / She	**was**	**doing** the laundry	_____		the door **opened**. the phone **rang**.
They / We	**were**	**studying**			

1 We use the Interrupted Past to show how a Simple Past action happened **before** / **in the middle of** a Past Progressive action.

2 We use both the Simple Past and the **Past** / **Present** Progressive to form the Interrupted Past.

Infinitives of purpose

__________	you / he / she / they	**go** the hospital? **make** a cake?
I / He / She / They	**went** to the hospital **made** a cake	**to see** the doctor. ________ **surprise** a friend.

3 We use Infinitives of purpose to describe **why** / **when** we did something.

4 We use an infinitive verb in the **first** / **second** part of the sentence.

2 Work with a partner to write a short story using the Interrupted Past. Choose one of these story openers.

The prince was gardening when ...

The astronaut was studying the moon when ...

I was blowing up balloons when ...

3 Discuss your story using Infinitives of Purpose. Ask and answer.

Why did the astronaut leave the spaceship?

He left the spaceship to pick up the trash.

Think!

Mrs. Khan's wrist hurts.

Grammar

8

1 Read and complete. Then read and circle.

does than many ~~would~~

Preferences

I / You / He / She / We / They	would **rather**	**listen to** jazz **eat** pizza **play** the piano **laugh**	______	pop. burgers. the violin. eat.

1 We use *would rather* to compare two **actions** / **nouns**.
2 We use *would rather* … **than** / **that** to compare two things.

***How* questions**

How	**long**	is the concert? is the movie?
	______	singers are there?
	much	does a ticket cost? ______ the cake cost?

3 We use *How long* to ask about **length of time** / **cost**.
4 We use a **verb** / **noun** after *How many …?*

2 How well do you know your partner? Write sentences with *would rather* and check.

You would rather play basketball than volleyball.

music food activities clothes pets

You get 100 points for each one you get right!
How many points can you and your partner get in five minutes?

☐ correct statements
☐ points

Think!

The musicians play the electric guitar, the keyboard, and the drums.

3 Ask and answer about the concerts you and your partner went to.

How many singers are there?

Student A

1 drummer	☐ musicians
4 dancers	☐ singers
90 minutes	$☐

Student B

☐ drummer	5 musicians
☐ dancers	2 singers
☐ minutes	$15

Grammar

1 Read and complete. Then read and circle.

might | herself | tie | +

by + reflexive pronouns

I	made the uniform put up the tent read the map went hiking	by	myself.
You			yourself.
He			himself.
She			________
We			ourselves.
They			themselves.

1 We use *by* + reflexive pronouns to talk about something done ***alone*** / ***to someone else***.

2 We put the reflexive pronoun at the **beginning** / **end** of the sentence.

***may / might / could* for possibility**

I / You / He / She / We / They	**may** ________ **could**	**go** canoeing. **explore** the Sahara Desert. **use** a compass. ________ a knot.

3 We use *may* / *might* / *could* to say something is **definite** / **possible**.

4 We use ***an infinitive*** / ***a past participle*** after *may* / *might* / *could*.

2 Write sentences about you using *by myself*.

I baked a cake by myself.
I put up a tent by myself.
I ...

3 Talk about what you could do on a vacation using *may*, *might*, and *could*. Compare with a partner.

I might visit my grandparents.

Me too!

Think!

Barbara's favorite book was Robinson Crusoe.

Pearson Education Limited
KAO Two
KAO Park
Hockham Way
Harlow, Essex
CM17 9SR
England
and Associated Companies throughout the world.

pearsonenglish.com

First published 2022
ISBN: 978-1-292-44172-6
Set in Arta Medium 16/18pt

Printed in Slovakia by Neografia

Acknowledgements:
The publishers and author would like to thank the following people for their feedback and comments during the development of the material: Maria Silvina Campagnoli, Maria Lidia Camporro, Maria Sol Diaz, Tatiana Fanshtein, Jiang Xin, Paula Mior, Anita Parlaj-Naranic, Marta Popiolek, Jelena Tosic.

Image Credits:
123RF.com: Belchonock 94, Daisydaisy 25, Fernando Gallardo 25, Kaspars Grinvalds 36, Lightfieldstudios 100, Maxpayne222 102, Picsfive 54, Ra2studio 35, Richard Villalon 84, Serezniy 84, Sergey Novikov 29, Tartila 68, Tlorna 53; **Alamy Stock Photo**: Album 78, B Christopher 72, Cavan Images 110, Cultura Creative RF 109, Cultural Archive 79, Massimo Salesi 79, Peter Horree 79; **Getty Images:** a_namenko/iStock/Getty Images Plus 29, Africalmages/E+ 85, Agustavop/E+ 116, Alfnqn/iStock/Getty Images Plus 116, Badmanproduction/iStock/Getty Images Plus 48, Bob Thomas/Popperfoto 112, Bonottomario/iStock/Getty Images Plus 103, Carol Yepes 35, Chrisinthai/iStock/Getty Images Plus 78, CynthisAnnF/iStock/Getty Images Plus 17, D.Sharon Pruitt Pink Sherbet Photography/Moment 53, Daniel Milchev 16, DaniloAndjus 77, Dbvirago/iStock/Getty Images Plus 78, Dean Mitchell 53, Deklofenak/iStock/Getty Images Plus 71, Difinbeker 33, Gannet77/iStock/Getty Images Plus 41, GarryKillian 114, Giannimarchetti/iStock/Getty Images Plus 79, Imcd/iStock/Getty Images Plus 84, Jaume Capella Villalonga/iStock/Getty Images 49, jilipko/iStock/Getty Images Plus 55, Kristoffer Alderstrand/EyeEm 88, Kyslynskyy/iStock/Getty Images Plus 19, Larisa_zorina 17, LightFieldStudios/iStock/Getty Images Plus 109, Ma-no/iStock/Getty Images Plus 48, MikeLane45/iStock/Getty Images Plus 19, NatashaPhoto/iStock/Getty Images Plus 54, Nikuwka/iStock/Getty Images Plus 52, Nirut Saelim/EyeEm 41, Peoplelmages/E+ 17, Peoplelmages/iStock/Getty Images Plus 85, Peter Dazeley/The Image Bank 32, Riou/Photodisc 48, Robert Landau/Corbis Documentary 60, SbytovaMN/iStock/Getty Images Plus 114, Schnuddel/E+ 102, SolStock/E+ 85, Stellalevi/E+ 64, THEPALMER/iStock/Getty Images Plus 17, Thomas Barwick/DigitalVision 19, Westend61 31, Windzepher/iStock/Getty Images Plus 109; **Pearson Education Ltd:** Jon Barlow: 8, 9, 12, 16, 20, 24, 28, 36, 40, 48, 52, 60, 64, 67, 72, 76, 84, 88, 95, 100, 108, 112, 118, 119, 120, 121, 122, 123,124, 125, 126, 127; **Shutterstock:** 2happy 54, Africa Studio 29, Alex Staroseltsev 113, Anton-Burakov 54, Antonio Guillem 65, Bltt24 29, Blacqbook 109, Bondar Ann 56, Chaosamran_Studio 90, CLIPAREA I Custom media 30, David W. Leindecker 103, Elena Shashkina 49, Eric Isselee 103, F9photos 114, Fanfo 56, Gelpi 18, Golbay 81, Graeme Dawes 48, Haveseen 67, Iakov Filimonov 76, Janniwet 93, Karamysh 17, Krakenimages.com 25, Lianys 59, LightField Studios 72, Marlon Lopez MMG1 Design 36, Morok 49, Motive56 102, mountainpix 72, Natali_ploskaya 84, Optimarc 9, 33, 45, 69, 105, 117, Oriontrail 102, Paffy 84, Patrick Foto 31, Polina LVT 53, Prapass 91, PrimeMockup 21, RAGMA IMAGES 70, Sandra van der Steen 84, Serhii Bobyk 61, ShotPrime Studio 49, Simoly 108, Stanislav Tiplyashin 25, STILLFX 105, Super8 113, Syda Productions 85, Tahalefty 55, TJ Armer 79, Valentyn Volkov 53, Veres Production 72, Vgreek 34, Zivica Kerkez 59, Zoomonpictures.it 85.

Illustrations
Andrea Castro Naranjo/Beehive Illustration pp. 19, 42, 54, 65, 90, 101, 114, 115; **Catharine Collingridge/The Bright Agency** pp. 98-99, 126; **Emily Cooksey/Plum Pudding** pp. 9, 44, 55, 116; **Charolotte Grange/Plum Pudding** pp. 38-39, 121; **Kristina Kister/The Bright Agency** pp. 26-27, 120; **Adam Linley/Beehive Illustration** pp. 37, 66, 90, 102; **Tiziana Longo/The Bright Agency** pp. 12, 24, 73; **Bethany Lord/Advocate Art** pp.52, 65, 68, 79, 96; **Giovana Medeiros/Advocate Art** pp. 29, 48, 60; **Dolo Okecki/Astound US** pp. 86-87, 125; **Davide Ortu/Beehive Illustration** pp. 74-75, 124; **Giulia Pallanca/Collaborate** pp. 13, 53, 92; **Max Rambaldi/Advocate Art** pp. 14-15, 119; **Daniel Rieley/The Bright Agency** pp. 110-111, 127; **Ana Sebastián/The Bright Agency** pp. 62-63, 123; **Simon Smith/Beehive Illustration** pp. 76; **Rhian Stone/Plum Pudding** pp. 50-51, 122; **Joe Wilkins/Beehive Illustration** pp. 9.